Edward Manning Ruttenber

Obstructions to the Navigation of Hudson's River

Embracing the minutes of the secret committee appointed by the Provincial

convention of New York, July 16, 1776, and other original documents relating to the

subject

Edward Manning Ruttenber

Obstructions to the Navigation of Hudson's River
Embracing the minutes of the secret committee appointed by the Provincial convention of New York, July 16, 1776, and other original documents relating to the subject

ISBN/EAN: 9783337377199

Printed in Europe, USA, Canada, Australia, Japan

Cover: Foto ©ninafisch / pixelio.de

More available books at **www.hansebooks.com**

OBSTRUCTIONS

TO THE

NAVIGATION

OF

HUDSON'S RIVER;

EMBRACING

The MINUTES of the 𝕾𝖊𝖈𝖗𝖊𝖙 𝕮𝖔𝖒𝖒𝖎𝖙𝖙𝖊𝖊
Appointed by the Provincial Convention of New York, July 16, 1776,

AND OTHER

Original Documents Relating to the Subject.

TOGETHER WITH

PAPERS RELATING TO THE BEACONS.

BY E. M. RUTTENBER.

ALBANY, N. Y.:
J. MUNSELL, 78 STATE STREET.
MDCCCLX.

TO

Samuel Holden Parsons, Esq.,

OF MIDDLETOWN, CONN.

SIR :

ROM among the Documentary Memorials, relating to the Occupation and Defence of the Highlands of the Hudfon during the Revolutionary War, there could fcarcely be felected any, of a more interefting Clafs, than thofe that afford Details of the Plans to prevent the Paffage of the armed Ships of the Enemy, by obftructing the Channel of the River. So long as an uninterrupted Communication could be maintained, between New England and the States South and Weft of the Hudfon, there was Opportunity for Coöperation, and a Hope of efficient Refults from Unity of Action. If this Communication could by any Means be cut off, the Enemy might reafonably hope to Conquer the revolting Colonies in Detail. The Prominence given to the Subject, both in the Continental and the Provincial Congreffes, and the various Meafures adopted with a View towards fecuring this important Pafs, are hiftoric-ally Interefting, as throwing new Light upon the Condition of Strategick Science and Military Skill, in the early Infancy of the Republick. Whilft, from the Study of the Details, we derive additional In-formation refpecting the Opinions of the Publick Men of the Day, the Spirit of the People, and the Refources of the Country. The Documents here firft collected, may, for thefe Reafons, juftly claim a Place among the treafured Mementos of the Heroick Age of our Annals.

With the Times and Events chronicled in thefe Pages, your diftinguifhed Grand-Father, Brigadier General Samuel H.

PARSONS, was intimately and prominently connected. He was the Commanding Officer at Weſt Point, when the Chief and beſt-known Obſtruction to the Paſſage of the Enemy's Veſſels (the Weſt-Point Chain), was in the Progreſs of Conſtruction. And thus, himſelf a Portion of the Events, it ſeems only fitting that his Name ſhould be cloſely aſſociated with the Work that commemorates them.

By inſcribing this Volume to you, Sir, his worthy Nameſake and Deſcendant, the Publiſher would expreſs his Reſpect for the Memory of the One, and his Eſteem for the Character of the Other.

CONTENTS.

INTRODUCTION.

HE Student of American Hiſtory is familiar with the Faɕ, that to obtain Control of the Navigation of Hudſon's River, was a favourite Projeɕ with the Britiſh Miniſtry, during the whole Progreſs of the War of Independence.

In order to a proper Underſtanding of the Rea-ſons on which this Projeɕ was baſed, we ſhould examine with ſome Attention the Topography of the River—not ſimply as limited to ·the Seɕion of Country through which its Waters flow, but taking a broader View, and regarding its Conneɕion with thoſe more remote and wide-ſpread Regions, that find through it their moſt direɕ and natural Chan-nel to the Seaboard.

A

Even at the prefent Day, when the fkilled Enterprife of a numerous and commercial People has
linked the Interiour to the Coaft, by many and various artificial Channels, the great Thoroughfare of
the State of New York holds a prëeminent Pofition—mainly due to its unrivalled natural Advantages. But thefe Advantages were of paramount
Importance, both before and during the Revolutionary Struggle, when the Canoe of the Indian, or
the Bateau of the *Voyageur*, furnifhed the moft
convenient and fpeedy Tranfportation, for Purpofes
either of Commerce or of War. Then, to the
North, at the Head of Boat-navigation, the Hudfon was connected, by an eafy Portage, with Lakes
George and Champlain; and through them with
the St. Lawrence—the great River of the Canadas.
Whilft, towards the Weft, its principal Affluent,
the Mohawk, gave eafy Accefs—fcarcely interrupted
by a few fhort Portages—to the Bafin of the great
Lakes, and to the magnificent River Syftem of the
Miffiffippi.

Thus eftablifhed by Nature as the main Artery,
connecting a vaft Network of interiour Water-com-
munications with the Atlantick, and draining the

Refources of almoft half a Continent, the Hudfon occupied a Pofition of the firft ftrategick Importance.

The Britifh Miniftry had been taught this Fact in the Courfe of the long Struggle between England and France, then but recently terminated. They knew, that by the Poffeffion of the Hudfon they could feparate the Eaftern Part of the Province of New York and the Provinces of New England from the Remainder of the Confederacy, and thus, by cutting off Communication between thefe Points, fpeedily reduce the Patriots to Subjection. Hence, in a Letter dated London, July 31ft, 1775, conveying to the Colonifts the Plan of Operations decided upon by the Miniftry, it is faid, that "their Defign is to get Poffeffion of New "York and Albany; to fill both of thefe Cities with "very ftrong Garrifons; to declare all Rebels who "do not join the King's Forces; to command the "Hudfon's and Eaft Rivers with a Number of fmall "Men-of-War and Cutters ftationed in different "Parts of it, fo as to cut off all Communication "by Water between New York and the Provinces "to the Northward of it, and between New York "and Albany, except for the King's Service, and to "prevent alfo all Communication between the City

"of New York and the Provinces of New Jerfey,
"Pennfylvania, and thofe to the Southward of them.
"By thefe Means," continues the Letter, "the Ad-
"miniftration and their Friends fancy that they
"fhall foon either ftarve out or retake the Garrifons
"of Crown Point and Ticonderoga, and open and
"maintain a fafe Intercourfe and Correfpondence
"between Quebeck, Albany and New York, and
"thereby afford the faireft Opportunity to their
"Soldiery and the Canadians, in conjunction with
"the Indians, to be procured by G. J.,[1] to make
"continual Irruptions into New Hampfhire, Maffa-
"chufetts and Connecticut, and fo diftract and divide
"the Provincial Forces, as to render it eafy for the
"Britifh Army at Bofton to defeat them, break the
"Spirits of the Maffachufetts People, depopulate
"their Country, and compel an abfolute Subjection
"to Great Britain."[2]

[1] Col. Guy Johnfon, a Son-in-Law of Sir Wm. Johnfon, Superintendent of Indian Affairs of the Province of New York. On the death of Sir William, Col. Johnfon was appointed to the vacant Office—a Pofition that gave him great Influence with the Indian Tribes. In the early Part of the Controverfy with England, he fucceeded in inducing a large Proportion of the Six Nations to engage in the Service of the King.

[2] Journal of the Provincial Congrefs of New York, 172.

But the Colonifts were equally familiar with the Importance of maintaining Poffeffion of the River. In a Report fubmitted by the Provincial Congrefs of New York to the Continental Congrefs, early in 1775, the Subject is thus treated: "If the Enemy " perfift in their Plan of fubjugating thefe States to " the Yoke of Great Britain, they muft, in Propor- " tion to their Knowledge of the Country, be more " and more convinced of the Neceffity of their " becoming Mafters of Hudfon's River, which will " give them the entire Command of the Water " Communication with the Indian Nations, effect- " ually prevent all Intercourfe between the Eaftern " and Southern Confederates, divide our Strength " and enfeeble every Effort for our common Pre- " fervation and Security. That this was their " original Plan, and that Gen¹. Carleton and Gen¹. " Howe flattered themfelves with the delufive " Hope of uniting their Forces at Albany, every " Intelligence confirms, and it appears to the Com- " mittee that they will not give up this grand Object " until they fhall finally relinquifh the Project of " enflaving America."[1]

[1] Jour. Prov. Conv. N. Y., 723.

With this brief Explanation of the nati
which gave to Hudfon's River the impo
tion which it occupied in the Struggle
pendence, and of the Plans adopted by th
to fecure its Control, we come to confid
the Means employed by the Colonifts
the Efforts of the Englifh. The genei
tions of the Continental Forces are amp
in our Hiftories—Ticonderoga, Saratoga
Point, are written on their Pages in Cc
Time can never dim. Still, there are n
of Intereft that have not been recordec
efpecially fo in regard to the Fortificati
Highlands and the Charader and Num
Obftructions to the Navigation of the F
fupply Details in reference to the latt
will be the leading Objed of this Paper,
from the Connexion exifting between
former, alfo, will be incidentally noticed.

The Plan of Operations adopted by th
while aiming at general Refults, imme
volved the Province of New York; and
Congrefs of that Province took early St
vent its Confummation. Prior to the R

the Letter of July 31ft, already quoted, the Provincial Congrefs had taken Aĉtion upon the Subjeĉt of fortifying the Highlands and obſtruĉting the Navigation of the River, and had invited the prompt Aĉtion of the Continental Congrefs. On the 25th May, 1775, the latter Body communicated to the former a Series of Refolutions in reference to the Defence of New York, one of which is as follows:

" *Refolved*, That a Poft be taken in the High-
" lands, on each Side of Hudfon's River, and Bat-
" teries ereĉted; * * * and that experienced
" Perfons be immediately fent to examine faid
" River, in order to difcover where it will be moft
" advifable and proper to obftruĉt the Navigation."[1]

This Refolution, together with the Others of the Series, received the Aĉtion of the Provincial Congrefs at its Seffion held May 30th, 1775, when the following Order was paffed:

" *Ordered*, That Col. Clinton and Mr. Tappan
" be a Committee (and that they take to their
" Affiftance fuch Perfons as they fhall think necef-
" fary,) to go to the Highlands and view the Banks
" of Hudfon's River there; and report to this Con-

[1] Jour. Prov. Cong., 16.

" grefs the moft proper Place for ere£
" more Fortifications; and likewife an
" the Expenfe of erecting the fame."[1]

This Committee made a Report on
June, 1775, in which they fuggefted th
of what were afterwards known as F(
and Montgomery. In their Report th

" Your Committee begs Leave to c
" they are informed that by Means of
" Booms, chained together on one Side (
" ready to be drawn acrofs, the Paffage c
" up to prevent any Veffel paffing or r

On the 16th of June, 1775, the Prov
grefs took this Suggeftion into Confid(
paffed the following Order:

" *Ordered,* That Col. Hoffman, Mr.
" McDougall, and Mr. Paulding be a
" to inquire into the Depth of Water i
" River, from the City of New Yor
" Windfor.".

We have fearched in vain for the Re
Committee; but it is not effential, a

1 Jour. Prov. Cong., 20.   3 Ib., 45.
2 Ib., 41.

Matter is fhown by the Report of a Committee fubfequently appointed for that Purpofe. On the 18th Auguft, 1775, the Provincial Congrefs paffed the following Refolution :

" *Refolved,* That the Fortifications formaly[1] or-
" dered by the Continental Congrefs,   *   *   *
" be immediately erected."

In Accordance with this Refolution, the Erection of Forts Clinton and Montgomery was immediately commenced, under the Supervifion of a Committee of the Provincial Congrefs, affifted by Mr. Bernard Romans,[2] the Engineer appointed for

[1] Thus printed in the *Journal;* but is written *formerly* in Original, in the Office of Secretary of State, at Albany.

[2] BERNARD ROMANS was born in Holland, but early in Life removed to England, where he ftudied the Profeffion of an Engineer. He was employed as fuch by the Britifh Government, fome Time before the Revolution, in her Southern American Provinces ; although the firft Notice that we find of him is in a Manufcript in Harvard Library, written by John Gerard Wil-

liam de Brahm[1] where he is mentioned as a Refident of Florida, from 1763 to 1771, as a Draughtfman. It alfo appears that, pre-

[1] We gathered this Fact from Mr. Fairbanks's recent *Hiftory of St. Auguftine,* p. 165, where the Author's Name is mifprinted John Gerard Williams de Bahm. Mr. J. L. Sibley, Librarian at Harvard, in a Letter relating to this Manufcript, fays that the Author has fubfcribed his Name John Gerar William de Brahm ; while a Copyift had written it in the fame Volume, William Gerard de Brahm ; the latter is alfo the Form in which it ftands on the Title Page of the Book he publifhed in connection with Bernard Romans on the Gulf Paffage.

the Purpofe by the Continental Cong
Suggeftions of the Committee of May 2

vious to his Employment in the
Capacity of Engineer for the Conftruction of Defences in the Highlands, he was in the Enjoyment of
a Penfion from the Britifh Crown,
of about £50 Sterling per Year,
as Botanift in Florida. From a
Paper on the Mariner's Compafs,
which he communicated to the
American Philofophical Society, we
learn that he was ftill at St. Auguftine
in 1773. *(Trans.* 11, 396.) In
1775 he publifhed in New York the
firft Volume of a Natural Hiftory of
Florida;[1] the fecond Volume, although announced as *in prefs,* we
do not find to have been iffued.
He alfo publifhed the fame Year, a
Map of the Seat of Civil War in
America. Whilft at the North he
became imbued with the revolu-
tionary Spirit, and the New York
Committee of Safety engaged his
Services as Engineer, at $50 per
Month, to conftruct Defences in the
Highlands. He entered upon the
Duties of that Office on the 29th
Auguft, 1775, with the Encourage-

ment, as he alleged,
fion in the Continent
the 18th of Septemb
his Plans and Eftim:
penfes of erecting th
tifications (4 Force'
111, 732–36), and of
for the Completion
£5000, the Ordnanc
The Committee, he
to employ him at a
the Pay of a Colon
tinental Army. C
October he applied
a Commiffion, wit
Colonel. While I
was pending the Co
came diffatiffied wit
ings, and the Ma
before the Contin
for their Decifion.
verfy refulted in the
Mr. Romans, and (
appointed to fill h
Correfpondence bei
the Committee is giv
nal of Provincial C
100–6.   On the 8
1776, he was com
tain of a Company

---

[1] See Title in full in Duycklnck's
Cyc. Am. Literature, 1, 303.

in regard to Obſtructing the Navigation of the
River, do not, however, appear to have been acted

Artillery,[1] deſtined for the Invaſion
of Canada as a Part of the Northern
Army. On the 18th of March,
he applied to the New York Committee of Safety for Pay up to the
Date of his new Commiſſion, ſtating
that the Time had expired in which
he was to have appeared at the
Head of his Company, which want
of Money prevented. The next
we learn of him, he was ſent back
from Canada to Albany to be tried,
in May, 1776 (4 *Am. Archives,*
vi, 413), for Miſconduct, "a String
of Complaints" having been lodged
againſt him; the Purport of which
was, that he countenanced, or failed
to diſcountenance, the Depredations
committed by his Men upon the
People of the Country which they
quartered in; and on the 27th July
following he was again tried for
ſome Difficulty with his Lieutenant.
The Reſult of theſe Trials does not
appear, but it is inferred that he

[1] The Names, Rank, Dates of Com-
miſſions and Times of Enliſtment of the
Officers and Privates of his Company,
from Feb. 8, to Nov. 28, 1776, when
encamped at Ticonderoga, may be found
in Saffell's *Records of the Revolution,* p. 178.

was honourably acquitted; for he
continued in the Service, and early
in November was deputed, by
Gen. Gates, to inſpect the Works
at Fort Anne and Skeneſborough,
the Condition of which he reported with much Ability; and in the
ſame Month, the Pennſylvania
Council of Safety directed that
he ſhould be furniſhed with ſuch
Materials as he might require to
perform an Experiment, in Order
to give a Specimen of his Skill in
deſtroying diſtant Objects by Fire.
(5 *Am. Archives,* iii.) Unfortun-
ately we do not find the Reſult of
this Experiment. In 1778 he
publiſhed at Hartford, Conn., the
firſt Volume of his Annals of the
Troubles in the Netherlands; and
the ſecond Volume[1] was Printed at

[1] As the Exiſtence of this ſecond Volume is often queſtioned, the exact Title is
here given: Annals | of the Troubles |
in the | Netherlands | from the | Acceſ-
ſion of Charles V | Emperor of Germany
| A proper and ſeaſonable Mirror for the
preſent Americans | collected and trans-
lated from the moſt approved Hiſtorians
in the Native Tongues | By Bernard
Romans | Vol. II | Hartford | Hudſon &
Goodwin | M.D.CC.LXXXII.

upon—farther than to order the Sur
tioned—until the subsequent Year (177(

the same Place in 1782. He also
published in England, in 1779, in
Connection with Capt. de Brahm, A
Compleat Pilot for the Gulf Passage,
a Subject which is treated of in his
Work upon Florida. On the 28th
Jan., 1779, he married Elizabeth
Whiting *(Certificate of Rev. Mark
Tucker)* of Wethersfield, Ct., who
died in New York, 12th May,
1848, aged 89 *(Memorandum by
Peter Force, Esq.).* Her Miniature,
beautifully painted by Romans, is
still preserved in the Family *(Dr.
Wm. Dolby of N. Y.).* We find
no other Trace of him except in the
Deposition of his Widow, made for
the Purpose of obtaining a Pension,
15th Oct., 1845, on File in the Pension Office at Washington, which,
divested of its legal Technicalities,
is substantially as follows: That he
continued in the Line of his Duty
as an Officer until 1780, about
eighteen Months after his Marriage,
when he was ordered to go to the
State of South Carolina, there to
join the Southern Army; that shortly
thereafter he sailed from New Haven or New London for the Place

of his Destination, I
with all on Board, w
the Passage by the B
ried to Montego Bay,
he was held in Cap
Close of the War :
the British Authoriti
Time, were applied
ment to deliver him u
which was declined
his Ability to do In
ish Interests; that h
by the British Autho
Pretext of sending
some Port in the Ur
was said to have died
though, from Circur
ing his Demise, his F
Reason to believe t
fully murdered. T
of his Widow for
rejected on the G:
Service performed b
ever meritorious,
tary, and therefore
for by the Pension L
Whiting, Esq., Com
a Diary of the pr
of his Life, he c
been the first Surve

on the 16th of July, a few Days after the Declaration of Independence, the Provincial Convention[1] again took up the Matter, and appointed a *Secret Committee* to take the whole Subject in charge; as will be feen by the following Refolutions :

" *Refolved, unanimoufly,* That a Secret Committee
" be appointed to devife and carry into Execution
" fuch Meafures as to them fhall appear moft
" Effectual for Obftructing the Channel of Hud-
" fon's River, or annoying the Enemy's Ships in
" their Paffage up faid River; and that this Con-
" vention Pledge themfelves for defraying the
" Charges incident thereto.

" *Refolved,* That Mr. Jay, Mr. Robert Yates,[2]

As a Mathematician, an Artift, an Author, or as a Publick Man, he feems to have been regarded by all, except the New York Committee of Safety, as a choice Spirit. He left one Son, Bernard Hubertus, who died near Havana of Yellow Fever, leaving an only Son of the fame Name.

[1] The Title of the Legiflature of the State was changed on the 10th July, 1776, from *Congrefs* to *Convention,* as follows : Refolved and

Ordered, that the Style or Title of this Houfe be changed from that of *The Provincial Congrefs of the Colony of New York,* to that of *The Convention of the Reprefentatives of the State of New York. (Journal,* 1, 519.)

[2] ROBERT YATES was born at Scheneftady, New York, 27th Jan., 1738, and became an eminent Lawyer in Albany; was a Member of the Board of Alderman in the latter City from 1771 to 1775;

" Major C. Tappan, Mr. Robert R. Liv
" Mr. Paulding be faid Committee."

At this Point the Congreffional and
Records ceafe to help us in our Inv
The Proceedings of the Provincial Con
indeed, make frequent References to th
tions, but they are brief and unfatisfact
furnifh no Means of identifying and un
the Objects and Events to which t
Fortunately, however, the Original Min
Proceedings of the Secret Committee
16th July, 1776, have been recently
by Mr. James C. Bolton, among the P
Grand-father, Gen. James Clinton. I
Minutes, Mr. Bolton has found Maps o
at Fort Montgomery, fhowing the Mann
it was faftened and floated, and the Char

wrote under the Signature *The*
Rough Hewer, under which *Sou-*
briquet he was known; was a
Member of the Provincial Con-
grefs from 1775 to 1777, and
Chairman of the Committee for
Military Operations; in 1777 was
appointed Judge of the Supreme
Court; and in 1790 Chief Juftice;

1788 was a Mem
vention which rati
Conftitution; was
Secret Proceedings
the Convention of
after his Death.
ticular Account of
Council of Revifion

Booms placed in Front of it; together with many other Papers of great Value relating to the Obftructions at Fort Wafhington and Pollopel's Ifland. Thefe long-hidden and valuable Documents receive additional Illuftration from a Relick of the Original Obftruction at Weft Point, which was raifed from the River's Bed, by Bifhop's Derrick, in 1855.[1] Collating and combining this Mafs of new and important Materials, with that to be derived from the Proceedings of the Provincial Convention, and from other previoufly known Sources, we find that a Flood of Light is thrown upon the Subject, enabling us to get a clear and complete Idea of it, in whole and in detail.

There were four Points at which it was fought to obftruct the Navigation of the River, by means, either fingly or combined, of *Fire Ships*, *Booms*, *Chains*, and *Chevaux-de-Frife.* The *Firft* was at

[1] This interefting Relick is now depofited at Wafhington's Head Quarters, Newburgh. It is the Property of E. Carter, Efq., of Newburgh, to whofe Exertions the Publick are mainly indebted for the valuable Collection of Manufcripts and Revolutionary Relicks now preferved in this old, temporary, Home of Wafhington. The Papers of Gen. James Clinton, referred to in the Text, have found a fitting refting Place in the fame Collection, having been there depofited by his Grand-fon, Mr. Bolton. Wafhington's Head Quarters was purchafed, feveral Years fince, by the State of New York, and is now under its efpecial Care and Protection.

Fort Wafhington, the *Second* at Fort Montgomery, the *Third* at Pollopel's Ifland, and the *Fourth* at Weft Point. The Fire Ships and Obftructions at Fort Wafhington were conftructed in the Summer of 1776; the Obftructions at Fort Montgomery and Pollopel's Ifland in the Autumn of 1776 and Springs of 1777 and 1778; and thofe at Weft Point in 1778. We propofe to notice thefe feveral Obftructions in their chronological Order.

I.

OBSTRUCTION

BY MEANS OF

FIRE SHIPS.

OBSTRUCTION

OF THE

NAVIGATION OF THE RIVER

BY MEANS OF

FIRE SHIPS AND RAFTS.

NTERIOR to the Appointment of the Secret Committee, there had been some Difcuffion, in reference to the Modes to be employed in obftructing the Navigation of the River. Among other Propofitions, the Plan of conftructing Fire Ships, or Rafts, which had been introduced by Capt. Hazelwood,[1] on the Delaware, was favorably received by the Convention; and it alfo met the Approval of both Gen. Wafhington and

[1] JOHN HAZELWOOD was a resident of the City of Philadelphia, and was employed by the Committee of Safety of that City, to whom he communicated the Plan of conftructing Fire Ships and Rafts for the

Gov. Clinton.[1] Early in July, 1776, Wafhington iffued Orders, to the Committee having Charge of the Conftruction of the Continental Frigates at Poughkeepfie, to equip a number of Fire Rafts and Veffels. In obedience to this Order, the Work was immediately commenced.[2]

On the Appointment of the Secret Committee,

Defence of the Delaware River. The Legiflature of Pennfylvania, at the Suggeftion of the Committee of Philadelphia, authorized the Conftruction of a Fleet of thefe Veffels, and gave him the Commiffion of Captain. He was fent to Poughkeepfie by the Committee of Safety of Philadelphia, for the Purpofe of Aiding the Secret Committee. (See *Letter from Wm. Duer* under head of Fort Wafhington.) After his Return from New York, he was raifed to the Rank of Commodore, by the Order of Gen. Greene, Oct. 7, 1777 (*Sparks*, v., 77), and rendered efficient Service at the Attack on Fort Mercer, Oct. 21, 1777, and in the fubfequent Operations on the Delaware River, and was honored by Congrefs with a Sword. His Fleet was difperfed at the Capture of Forts Mercer and Mifflin, Nov. 21, 1777.

1   " FORT CONSTITUTION,
        " July 14, 1776.
"I Approve of much of your " Plan for making Fire Rafts, and " doubt not you will carry the fame " into Execution with the utmoft

" Expedition. I think it advifable " to purchafe two other old Sloops, " or more, if neceffary, for the " Purpofe, but let it be done in " the cheapeft Manner — the old- " eft and worft Sloops will do. * * " GEO. CLINTON.
" To Secret Committee."
(Clinton Papers, State Lib.)

2   " POUGHKEEPSIE,
        " July 16, 1776.
" As you were pleafed to for- " ward us Genl. Wafhington's Or- " ders to complete a Number of " Fire Rafts and Fire Veffels, we " have the Pleafure to inform you " that four Fire Rafts will be " launched this Evening. To- " morrow, we propofe to fix them " in the beft Manner we can with " dry Wood, Tar and fuch other " Combuftibles as we can procure " at this Place. Two or three old " Veffels we fhall fix as faft as poffi- " ble for the fame Purpofe. We " fhall fend the Fire Rafts down to " Col. Clinton as foon as com- " pleted." * * * * * *
(Letter from J. Van Zandt to Gov. Clinton.)

however, the Conſtruction of Fire Ships paſſed into their Hands; and in their Minutes of July 25th, we find the following, among other Inſtructions iſſued to the Artizans and Agents employed by them:

" 2d. The Building and Fitting out *ten* Fire " Rafts, and Preparing ſuch Veſſels as they may be " furniſhed with for Fire Ships, and ſending the " Same down to Fort Conſtitution as ſoon as made. " Alſo 12 Fire Grappling Irons.[1]

* * * * * * * * *

" 4th. To get 1000 Fire Arrows made and " fixed."

At the Meeting of the Committee on the 27th, the following Memorandum of Articles to be procured was entered in the Minutes:

" Light Wood and Pine Knots for Fire Veſſels, " to be got at Eſopus and Albany.

" Mr. Tappan to procure three old Sloops and " ſend them down to Poughkeepſie loaded with " thoſe Knots and Light Wood, and as much " Pitch, Tar, Turpentine, and Tar-Tubs and Bar- " rels, as can be got.

" Mr. Livingſton and Mr. Yates to procure the " ſame Number of Sloops and to ſend them down

[1] The Grappling Iron has Radiating Hooks at the end, intended to catch in the Rigging of an enemy's Veſſel, and thus faſten the Fire Ship alongſide.

"loaded with the ſame Materials. The Pitch,
"Tar, and Turpentine not to exceed 100 Barrels.
"Alſo, Oakum and Junks[1] of Rope. Alſo, to
"Procure 100 Aſh Oars from 14 to 20 feet long.

"Mr. G. Livingſton to procure ſix Long Boats
"and ſend them to Poughkeepſie. To get about
"twelve Fire Grappling Irons made. To get
"1000 Fire Arrows made. To fit up one or two
"armed Sloops at Albany. To ſend to Saliſbury
"for all the Cannon and all the Shot that can be
"procured there."

The Plan evidently was, to draw theſe Rafts acroſs
the River in a Line.[2] The Fire Arrows were Intended to be diſcharged in ſuch Manner as to
communicate Fire to the Sails of approaching
Veſſels, while the Fire Rafts were to be cut from
their Moorings and propelled againſt their Hulls.
The Combuſtibles being ſimultaneouſly ignited, the
Veſſels aſſailed would almoſt inſtantly be wrapped in
Flames. The Fire Ships were charged under the
Direƈtion of Capt. Hazelwood, whoſe Services in
this Reſpeƈt will be found detailed in the following
Certificate, which alſo contains a Liſt of the Mate-
rials uſed by him:

---

[1] Junk is old Rope, cut into ſhort lengths.

[2] "Auguſt 2, 1776. This Day "ſome of the Carpenters from "Poughkeepſie arrived with the "Fire Rafts, and To-morrow or "next Day hope to be able to "draw them across the River." *(Mem. by Gov. Clinton.)*

" Poughkeepsie, Aug. 26th, 1776.

" 2 Brls of Spirits of Turpentine.

" 6 gals. of Spirit of Wine.

" 60 Hand Grenade Shells complete.

" 12 ftrong Port Fires.

" 10 lbs. Slow Matches.

" 10 lbs. Spun Cotton.

" The feveral Articles mentioned in the above
" Lift, were brought up here by Capt. Hazelwood
" to Poughkeepfie, part of which Articles have
" been ufed by him in charging a Fire Veffel here
" and left the Remainder for that Ufe."

" CHRISTR. TAPPEN.

" GILBERT LIVINGSTON.

" Copy,"

Having charged one Veffel, and given proper
Inftrudions as to the Manner of charging the others,
Capt. Hazelwood left Poughkeepfie. The Secret
Committee certified to his Services as follows :

" POUGHKEEPSIE, Aug, 26, 1776.

" SIR :

" Captain Hazelwood, who came up to us
" by Requeft of Convention, has fitted a Fire Vef-
" fel, as we Conceive in a Mafterly Manner, and
" has given fuch Inftrudions to fome Perfons we
" have here employed with refpedt to mixing Fire
" Combuftibles, &c., that we think we can now

" carry on our Works without further Assistance,"
&c.

" CHRISTR. TAPPEN.
" GILBERT LIVINGSTON.
" To ABM. YATES,
        " Pres't Provincial Congress."

At a Meeting of the Convention held August
29th, 1776, the following Resolution passed:

" The Convention having been informed by
" their Secret Committee of the Service of Capt.
" Hazelwood, in preparing Fire Rafts, and giving
" useful Information relative to the Obstructing the
" Navigation of Hudson's River, think him entitled
" to the Thanks of this House : and as a Compen-
" sation for his Expenses and Trouble,

" *Ordered,* That the Treasurer of this Conven-
" tion pay to the said Captaine Hazelwood, three
" hundred Dollars," &c.

The Fire Ships were subjected to an early Test.
The British Frigates *Rose* and *Phœnix* having
passed, in July, the Obstructions at Fort Washington, and ascended the River as far as Yonkers, it
was agreed upon that they should be attacked.
The Night of the 16th of August was selected for
the Purpose.   The Action was witnessed, from
the High Grounds at Yonkers, by Gen. Heath,
Gen. Clinton, and Others, and it is thus described
in Heath's Memoirs :

On the Evening of Aug. 16th, Gen. Heath,
accompanied by Gen. Clinton and other Officers,
took a proper Pofition on the Bank of the Hudfon.
" The Night," fays Heath himfelf, " was pretty
" dark ; we foon found that the Gallies and Fire
" Veffels were filently moving up with the Tide.
" After fome Time, and almoft immediately after
" the Sentinels on Board the Englifh Ships had
" paffed the Word, ' All is well,' two of the Fire
" Veffels flafhed into a Blaze ; the One clofe on the
" fide of the Phœnix, and the Other grappling one
" of the Tenders. To Appearances, the Flames
" were againft the fide of the Phœnix ; and there
" was much Confufion on Board. A Number of
" Cannon were difcharged into the Fire Veffel in
" order to fink her. A Number of Seamen af-
" cended and got out on the Yard-Arm, fuppofed
" to clear away fome of the Grapplings. The Fire
" Veffel was along fide, as was judged, near Ten
" Minutes, when the Phœnix either cut or flipped
" her Cables, let fall her Fore Top Sail, wore round
" and ftood up the River, being immediately veiled
" from the Spectators by the Darknefs of the Night.
" The Rofe and the other two Tenders remained at
" their Moorings."

Additional Particulars in Reference to the
Tranfaction are given in the following Letter from
Gen. Wafhington to Gov. Trumbull,[1] under Date
of Auguft 18th :

[1] Sparks, iv, 54.

* * " On the Night of the 16th, two of our
" Fire Veffels attempted to burn the Ships of War
" up the River.   One of thefe boarded the Phœnix
" of Forty-Four Guns, and was Grappled with her
" for fome Minutes, but unluckily fhe cleared her-
" felf.   The only Damage the Enemy fuftained
" was the Deftruction of one Tender.   It is agreed
" on all Hands, that our People engaged in this
" Affair, behaved with great Refolution and Intre-
" pidity.   One of the Captains, Thomas, it is to
" be feared, perifhed in the attempt or in making
" his Efcape by Swimming, as he has not been
" heard of.   His Bravery entitled him to a better
" Fate.   Though this Enterprife did not fucceed
" to our Wifhes, I incline to think it alarmed the
" Enemy greatly; for this Morning the Phœnix
" and Rofe, with their Two remaining Tenders,
" taking advantage of a brifk and profperous Gale
" and favorable Tide, quitted their Stations, and
" have returned and joined the reft of the Fleet."

The Veffels were confiderably injured in their
downward Paffage, in paffing the American Batteries
at Fort Wafhington and Harlem River.   The Tender, which had been burnt by the Fire Ships, was
towed down to the Fort the Day after the Affair,
although under the Fire of the Enemy's Cannon.
This was effected by a Lieutenant and two Men,
in a Manner that reflected great Credit upon their
Enterprife and Courage.   A Six-pounder Cannon,

three fmaller ones, and ten Swivels were taken out of the Tender.

A full Account of the Manner in which the Fire Ships were charged, and alfo of the Attack on the Britifh Frigates, was publifhed in the *Worcefter Magazine*, in 1826, in a Sketch of the Life of Jofeph Bafs, of Leicefter. It will fittingly conclude this Divifion of our Subject. Mr. Bafs ftates that at the Time of the Occurrence he was attached to the Water Service, under the Command of Commodore Tupper, who was directed to man the Fire Ships defignated for the Service. The Commodore felected Bafs to take Charge of one, and put the other under the Command of Captain Thomas, who belonged to New London. The Veffel commanded by Bafs was a Sloop, called the Polly, of about one hundred Tons burthen, nearly new. That commanded by Thomas, was of a fmaller Size. The Frigates lay about eight Miles above Kingfbridge, but having had Intimations that they might be attacked, removed their Station towards the weftern Shore of the River, where the Water was deeper than on the eaft Side.

The Fire Ships had been prepared with Faggots of the moft combuftible Kinds of Wood, which had been dipped in melted Pitch, and with Bundles of Straw cut, about a Foot long, prepared in the fame Manner. Thefe Faggots and Bundles filled the Deck and Hold as far aft as the Cabin; and into this Mafs of combuftible Materials was inferted a

Match, that might be fired by a Perſon in the
Cabin ; who would have Time to eſcape, through
a Door cut in the Side of the Veſſel, into a Whale
Boat that was laſhed to the Quarter of the Sloop.
Beſides theſe Combuſtibles, there were in each
Veſſel ten or twelve Barrels of Pitch. A quantity of
Canvaſs, amounting to many Yards, was cut into
Strips, about a Foot in Width, then dipped in
Spirits of Turpentine and hung upon the Spars and
Rigging, extending down to the Deck. Every
thing had been ſo prepared that but a Moment's
Time was required to ſet the whole Veſſel in a
Blaze.

The Fire Ships ſtarted from the Spuyten Duyvel
Creek about Dark, with a ſouth Wind and a favorable Tide. The Night was Cloudy and Dark, with
occaſionally a little Rain. Bals had nine Men attached to his Veſſel, three of whom he ſtationed
in the Whale Boat, four had Charge of the Grappling Irons, and one acted as Pilot, while Bafs ſtationed himſelf in the Cabin to fire the Materials.

Beſides the two Britiſh Frigates, there was a
Bomb Ketch and two Tenders; which were moored
near them. They were anchored in a Line about
North and South ; firſt the Phœnix of about 44
Guns; next the Roſe of 36 Guns; then the Bomb
Ketch, and above it the Tenders. As the Night
was Dark, and the Fire Ships kept near the Middle
of the River, they were not aware that they were
near the Britiſh Veſſels, until they heard, immedi-

ately on their Left, the ftriking of the Bells, and
the Cry of the Sentinel's, *all's well.* It was twelve
o'Clock, and little did thofe who were flumbering
there imagine the Deftruction that hung over them.
The Shore was bold and rofe above the Mafts ;
and, in its dark Shadow, the Americans could
not diftinguifh the Situations of the Veffels, neither
could they afcertain their Size, or which of them
were Frigates. Bafs was a confiderable Diftance
in Advance of Thomas, and, upon hearing the
Cry of the Sentinels, he immediately bore down
upon the Line of the Britifh Fleet. He was
already very near the Bomb Ketch before he was
difcovered by the Enemy, and foon ftruck her.
The Grappling Irons were made faft in an Inftant—
the Whale Boat was ready to caft off—the Match
was applied, and both Veffels were almoft immediately in a Blaze. Bafs and his Crew made their
way to the Shore, while the Panic-ftruck Crew of
the Ketch were feen pouring from their Quarters
in the utmoft Confternation. Several of them
perifhed in the Flames, others jumped into the
Water, and were refcued by the other Veffels of the
Fleet; and the Ketch foon burned fo as to part
from her Moorings, when fhe drifted on Shore, and
was confumed to the Water's Edge.

Capt. Thomas was not fo fortunate. He was far
in the Rear, and the Light from Bafs's Ship fhowed
his Pofition to the Enemy ; who opened a vigorous
Cannonade and prepared themfelves to meet the

Attack.   But, nothing daunted by being difcovered, he bore down on the Phœnix, and became
grappled with her.   He then applied the Match to
the Combuftibles, but in fuch a way that his retreat
to the Boat was cut off, and he was obliged to leap
overboard to efcape the Flames.   Five of his Men
were compelled to follow his Example, and not
being able to reach the Boat, all perifhed in the
Water.

Notwithftanding the Phœnix was on Fire in
jeveral Places, fhe was faved from Deftruction by
cutting away Portions of her Rigging, and flipping
her Cables.   In the Attack, the Enemy loft nearly
feventy Men, befides fome Women and Children
who were on board the Ketch.

Although there are, in Official Documents, fome
farther Allufions to the Fire Ships, they appear to
have been found impracticable, as their Ufe was
foon after abandoned.   On the 5th Sept., 1776,
Mr. Duane, from a Committee appointed to vifit
the Highlands and examine the State of Defences
there, reported, among other things, " That the
" Fire Rafts are in fuch a State as not to be fit for
" ufe, having in part, Water in them ; and that the
" General (Clinton) does not know what to do
" with them."   Their Deftruction was probably
completed at the reduction of the Forts in October ;
and as Experience had not proved that their ufe
was practicable, none were fitted out afterwards.

II.

OBSTRUCTION

AT

FORT WASHINGTON.

THE

OBSTRUCTIONS

AT

FORT WASHINGTON.

HE Obftruftions to the Navigation of Hudfon's River at Fort Wafhington are almoft entirely loft Sight of in the general Hiftories of the Revolution. This is probably due to the Faft that they were placed there in the moft fecret Manner; and that all the Preparations connefted with them, were *covered under the Defign of obftrufting the Eaft River.* Forming, as they did, an important Part in the Plans for the Defeat of the Enemy, and for the Defence of New York, they were, however, regarded as of the moft urgent Neceffity. The following Letter from Mr. Duer to the Secret Com-

E

mittee, which we find among the Clinton Papers, reveals the Facts here ſtated:

"WHITE PLAINS, Sunday 21ſt July, 1776.
"DEAR GENTL:
     "I have juſt arrived at this Place from New
"York where I have converſed with Genl. Waſh-
"ington on the Purport of the Letter from the
"Secret Committee.[1]

     "Gens. Putnam and Mifflen have made an exact
"Survey of the River oppoſite Mount Waſhington

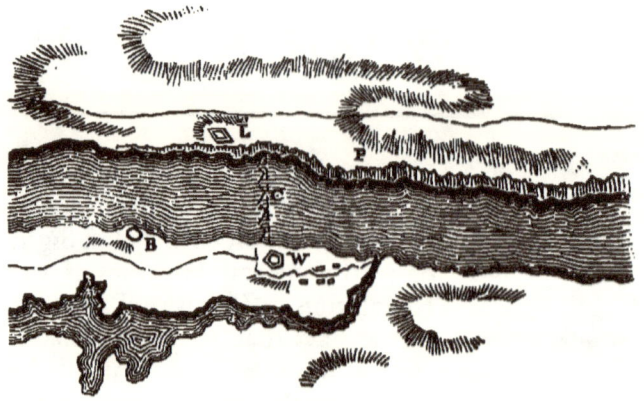

B—Bloomingdale.   W—Fort Waſhington.   L—Fort Lee.   P—Paliſades.
                       C—Chevaux-de-frize.

"and find that the Depth in no Part exceeds ſeven
"Fathoms; the Width, however, of the Channel
"(which is from three to ſeven Fathoms) is not
"much leſs than 1800 Yards, the ſhallow Part of

---

[1] The Draft of this Letter is not in the Collection of Manuſcripts.

" the River running in an oblique Direction. Genl.
" Wafhington expreffes himfelf extremely anxious
" about the Obftruction of that Channel, and
" Meafures are daily ufed for executing that Pur-
" pofe. It is impoffible to procure Veffels enough
" at New York, fo that the Meafure muft be de-
" layed till fuch Time as more Veffels can be
" brought through the Sound from Connecticut;
" however, I am not without Apprehenfions that
" this Refource will be cut off, as I underftand that
" fome of the Enemy's Veffels have failed out of
" the Hook, with an Intention (probably) of cutting
" off our Communication with the Sound.

" It is, however, an Object of fo much Import-
" ance that no Difficulties, however great, ought
" to deter us from our Attempts to carry it into
" execution ; *if we fucceed, the Defigns of the Enemy*
" *in this Campaign are effectually baffled*—if we fail,
" we cannot be in a more lamentable Situation than
" we are now.

" Exclufive of the great Advantage we fhould
" reap in obftructing the Channel fo far to the
" fouthward, it is, I fear, the only Place we can
" depend upon fhallowing[1] to the fouthward of the
" Highlands, whilft the Men-of-War are in the
" River, for if proper Batteries are erected near the
" Water at Mount Wafhington, and on the oppofite
" Side, mounted with Guns of 18, 24 and 32 Pound-

---

[1] Sufficiently fhallow.

" ers, it will not be practicable for any Veſſels to be
" ſo near as to prevent our working under the
" Cover of theſe Works. I have ſtrongly urged
" Genl. Waſhington to ſend Genl. Mifflen ſome
" heavier Metal, and he ſeems half inclined. This
" neceſſary Operation has not yet taken Place.

" The Genl. is anxious to have either of you
" (as Members of the Secret Committee) to be
" with him in Town, and has authorized me to
" make the Offer to you of his Houſe during your
" Reſidence. Let me entreat One of you imme-
" diately to come Down, and not to quit Genl.
" Waſhington till ſuch Time as this Meaſure on
" which our Safety depends is effected. There is
" ſuch a Languor and Procraſtination in our mili-
" tary Operations in that City and the true Object
" of this appears to me ſo much miſtaken, that I
" am confident either of your Preſences, in Order
" to preſs on the Obſtructions of that Channel,
" will be highly uſeful. There is another Con-
" ſideration which I hope will induce one of you
" to repair immediately to New York. The Com-
" mittee of Safety of Philadelphia have ſent three
" Perſons to New York in Order to aſſiſt us in
" making Fire Ships—one of them, a Mr. Hazel-
" wood, with whom I have converſed is particu-
" larly Clever. The Fire Ships charged in his
" Manner muſt, I am confident, prove Deſtructive
" to any Veſſel they fix upon. I have ſpoken con-
" cerning our Wiſh to deſtroy the Phœnix and

" Rofe, now in this River, and he is ready to
" undertake it, not doubting but he will meet with
" generous Encouragement. I applied to Genl.
" Wafhington to get Leave for him to come up
" the River; but his Prefence will ftill be wanted
" in Town, for the Ships there Loading, till this
" Day Week, when he will wait on your Com-
" mittee if you fend him Notice by Exprefs. He
" Lodges at Mrs. Graham's in Broad Street. I
" flatter myfelf, however, that either one or the
" other of you will fet off for Town immediately
" on the receipt of this Letter, in which cafe you
" can engage him in our Service, and fend him up
" immediately with the neceffary Apparatus.

" For News, I muft refer you to Mr. Paulding
" who left New York at the fame Time with my-
" felf. I fhall fet off for Connecticut To-Morrow
" where I think my Prefence is Neceffary. No
" more than 1900 of the Connecticut Quota had
" joined our Forces when I left Town.

" I had almoft forgot to tell you that this Defign
" of obftructing the Channel near Mifflin's *is cov-*
" *ered under the Pretext of preparing Veffels for*
" *obftructing the Channel of Eaft River.* It will,
" therefore, be advifable that your Converfation
" fhould give a Coloring to this Matter.

" I am, very Sincerely, yours, &c.,
" WM. DUER."

" P. S. For God's fake exert yourfelf to fecure
" the Sea Veffels which are in the River."

The Obſtructions, at this Point, were placed acroſs the River, between Forts Waſhington and Lee, and under the Command of their Guns, and were Completed only a ſhort Time before the Reduction of the former Fort by the Engliſh, on the 16th of November, 1776. They were made principally under the Direction of Perſons in the Employ of the Continental Congreſs, although Originally commenced by the Convention of the State of New York. Material Aid in their Conſtruction was contributed by the Secret Committee.

In the *Journal of the Provincial Convention,* we find that theſe Obſtructions received the Attention of that Body in the early Part of the Year 1776. It was then determined to obſtruct the Navigation of the River at this Point by *Chevaux-de-Frize,* and the Work of their Conſtruction was immediately commenced, and ſome of them ſent down and ſunk.

For the purpoſe of haſtening the completion of the Obſtructions, however, Gen. Putnam propoſed the Plan of ſinking Ships. This Plan is briefly Stated in a Letter from Gen. Putnam to Gen. Gates, dated July 26, 1776,[1] as follows :

＊＊ " We are preparing *Chevaux-de-Frize,* at " which we make great Deſpatch by the Help of " Ships, which are to be ſunk ; a Scheme of Mine, " which you may be aſſured is very Simple, a Plan " of which I ſend you. The two Ships' Sterns lie

---

[1] Sparks' iv, 30.

" towards each other, about feventy Feet apart.
" Three large Logs, which reach from Ship to
" Ship, are faftened to them. The two Ships and
" Logs ftop the River two hundred and eighty
" Feet. The Ships are to be funk, and, when
" hauled down on one fide, the Picks will be raifed
" to a proper Height, and they muft inevitably ftop
" the River, if the Enemy will let us fink them."

Finding the depth of the Water greater than
had been fuppofed, however, the Work was abandoned, and fome of the Frames of the *Chevaux-
de-Frize* firft funk were permitted to float up from
their places. On the 12th September, 1776, the
Convention called the Attention of Gen. Clinton
to the Matter, as follows :

" *Ordered,* That Robt. Harper prepare a Draft
" of a Letter to Gen. Geo. Clinton, requefting
" him to inform the Convention of the State of
" the *Chevaux-de-Frize* and other Obftructions to
" the Navigation of the River oppofite to Fort
" Wafhington."

Mr. Harper drafted the Letter accordingly. It
was as follows :

" SIR :
" Being informed by a Member of the Con-
" vention, that fome of the *Cheveaux-de-Frize* in-
" tended to be effectually funk in Hudfon's River,
" were a few Days ago floating with the Tide, I
" am Directed to requeft the Favor of you to in-
" form me what Probability there is of the Per-

" manence of thofe Machines, their Diftance, and
" whether you conceive the Navigation of the
" Enemy's Fleet is thereby Obftructed.

" I am, Sir, &c.,

" Robt. Harper.

" To Gen. Geo. Clinton."

Gen. Clinton's reply to this Letter we have not
been able to find; but it is not Effential. At its
Seffion on the 17th of that Month, the Convention, in a Preamble and Refolution, doubted the
Correctnefs of the Soundings which had been made
in the River at Fort Wafhington, and directed
Capt. Thos. Greenhill to retake the fame, and to
conduct the " Matter with all the *Secrefy* poffible."
The Report of Capt. Greenhill does not appear,
and as there is nothing in the Proceedings of the
Convention indicating that the Work was afterwards under its Direction, it is to be prefumed that
the duty of completing the Obftructions paffed
over to the Continental Authorities, or more
directly to Gen. Wafhington, who was at that
time making Arrangements for the Defence of
New York City.

On the 20th September, 1776, Gen. Wafhington, anticipating an Attack from the Britifh Veffels of War at New York, fent a Requeft to the
Convention, that they would fend to Fort Wafhington fome of the Fire Ships which had been
prepared by Capt. Hazelwood, where they would
" be Ready to Act in cafe the Ships fhould Attempt

" to come up." In accordance with this Requeſt, the Convention, on the 21ſt Sept., paſſed the following Order :

" *Ordered*, That Gilbert Livingſton, Eſq., or any " other Member of the Committee who may be " now at Poughkeepſie, do immediately diſpatch " the two Fire Ships, prepared and charged by " Capt. Hazlewood, with proper Perſons to navi- " gate them, under the Cover of the Guns of the " ſaid Fort, and there deliver them to the Care of " ſuch Perſon as His Excellency Gen. Waſhington " has or ſhall appoint to take Charge of them."

At this Seſſion of the Convention, a Letter from the Quarter-Maſter General to Capt. Cook was read, in which the latter was directed " to purchaſe " and procure Timber and oak Plank, with all poſ- " ſible Diſpatch, for the Uſe of the Army ;" and alſo " to purchaſe Veſſels, or take them at an Ap- " praiſement, for completing the Obſtructions to " the Navigation of Hudſon's River oppoſite to " Mount Waſhington." The Convention appointed a Committee to confer with Capt. Cook for the Purpoſe of aſcertaining what Aid " he ex- " pected of the Convention in the Premiſes." As the Reſult of this Conference the Committee reported the following Reſolutions, which were adopted by the Convention, viz :

" *Reſolved*, That the Secret Committee for ob- " ſtructing the Navigation of Hudſon's River be " empowered and directed to purchaſe or impreſs

F

" for the Service of the State any Number of Vef-
" fels not exceeding fix, which they fhall think beft
" calculated for the Purpofe of completing the
" Obftructions in the Hudfon's River oppofite to
" Mount Wafhington—that they caufe an Ap-
" praifement of the faid Veffels to be made by
" Perfons under Oath, in the moft equitable and
" expeditious Manner poffible in order that Satif-
" faction may be hereafter made by this Conven-
" tion to the Owners of fuch Veffels; and it is
" recommended to the faid Committee to requeft
" the Services of Capt. Thomas Grenell in ballaft-
" ing, navigating and delivering thofe Veffels to
" Capt. Cooke at Fort Wafhington.

" *Refolved*, That the faid Committee be directed
" to fend all the Oak Plank which they may have
" in their Poffeffion, to Mount Wafhington with
" the utmoft Difpatch."

Up to the Time of the Paffage of thefe Refolutions, the Secret Committee do not appear to have
had any Connection with the Obftructions at Fort
Wafhington, their Attention having been entirely
given to thofe at Fort Montgomery. On the Receipt of thefe Orders, however, the Committee
proceeded to execute them, as is fhown by their
Minutes :

" Poughkeepsie, Sept. 23d, 1776.
" At a Meeting of the Secret Committee of the
" Convention of the State of New York: Pre-
" fent, Robert Yates, Chn., Mr. Wifner, Mr.
" Livingfton, Mr. Harper.
" The Convention of this State, by their Refolve
" of the 21ft Inft., have empowered this Committee
" to purchafe or imprefs a Number of Veffels, not
" exceeding fix, to complete the Obftructions in
" Hudfon's River near Mount Wafhington, and to
" requeft the Services of Capt. Grenell in navigat-
" ing thofe Veffels down.

" By another Refolve of the fame Date, the
" Superintendants for building the Frigate are re-
" quefted to fend their fhort Plank to the fame
" Place ; and

" By a third Refolve of the fame Date, the faid
" Committee are requefted to fend down two Fire
" Ships charged by Capt. Hazlewood to the fame
" Place.

" The Committee having taken the fame into
" Confideration do Refolve immediately to fend
" down the Fire Veffel Mary Anna, and to requeft
" the Superintendant of the Shipyards to fpare a
" few Hands for navigating her.

" *Refolved*, That Capt. Cafewell load the Sloop
" Cambden with all fuch Plank as can be fpared at
" the Yards, and carry the fame down to Spiten-
" Devil—and that the Superintendants be requefted
" (purfuant to the Refolve of Convention), to give
" him all the Plank out of the Yards which can be

" spared.   That a Letter be wrote to Mr. Moylan,
" the Quarter-Master General, requesting him to
" pay for the Plank, &c.

" *Resolved*, farther, That the Sloop Clinton, pur-
" chased by this Committee be sent down to Mount
" Washington in order to be sunk there for obstruct-
" ing the Channel ; and that the Superintendants
" of the Yards be requested to furnish Men and
" Necessaries to navigate her down.

" *Resolved*, That another of the Fire Vessels
" down in the Highlands be sent down to the same
" Place.

" *Resolved*, That we have agreed to take up the
" two Brigs lying here, and the two large Ships at
" Esopus.

" It is the Advice and Opinion of Capt. Grenell,
" that we dispatch the two Brigs to Fort Washing-
" ton with such Men as may be had here, and that
" such other Men as are more Skillful in Naviga-
" tion, that we should take them to navigate the
" two large Ships at Esopus."

The next Meeting of the Committee was held
at Poughkeepsie, September 25th, 1776, of which
the following are the Minutes :

" At a Meeting of the Secret Committee : Present,
  " Robert Yates, Chn., Henry Wisner, Gilbert
  " Livingston, Robt. Harper.

" This Committee, pursuant to their Resolves
" and in consequence of the Power vested in them
" by the Convention of the State of New York,
" have impressed for the Use of the Publick two

" new Ships, the Property of Meffrs. Franklin,
" which were found near Efopus Landing—a
" Brig belonging to Meffrs. Malcom, Kip and
" others, at Poughkeepfie Landing, and another
" Brig lying at Schenck's Wharf, [probably Fifh-
" kill] owned (as is faid) by Lathrop and others in
" New England.

" And, in order that the Value of thefe Veffels
" refpectively may be afcertained, fo that the Own-
" ers may receive from the Publick a juft and
" equitable Compenfation,

" *Refolved*, That Auftin Lawrence, Saml. Tudor,
" Thos. Grenell, Stephen Simmons, Lancafter Bur-
" ling, Thos. Ives and David Stoddard be appointed,
" and they, or a Majority of them, are hereby ap-
" pointed Appraifers for the Purpofe of eftimating
" the Value of thofe Veffels, together with their
" Apparel and Furniture.

" *Refolved*, further, That the faid Appraifers,
" previous to their making fuch Appraifement, take
" the following Oath:

" You fwear that you will, to the beft of your
" Skill and Underftanding, juftly and impartially
" appraife the Value of the feveral and refpective
" Veffels, their Tackle and Furniture above men-
" tioned."

" And, *Refolved*, further, That the faid Appraif-
" ers or a Majority of them, be requefted, after
" fuch Appraifement is made, to reduce the fame to
" Writing under their Hands, in order to furnifh
" this Committee therewith."

Minutes of a Meeting on the 26th of September are among the Papers, but as the Proceedings have no direct Reference to either of the Obstructions, we have not copied them. On the 27th of September, the Appraisers submitted their Return. The Minutes are as follows:

"POUGHKEEPSIE, Sept. 27, 1776.

" At a Meeting of the Secret Committee: Present,
" Robt. Yates, Chn., Henry Wisner, Robt. Har-
" per, Jacob Cuyler.

" By the Return of the Appraisers it appears they
" have appraised

" The Brig of Lothrop and others,	£400
" The Brig of Malcom and others,	760
" The Ship of John Franklin,	3429
" The Ship of Samuel Franklin,	2800
" Total,	£7389

"*Resolved*, That Instructions be given to Capt. " North for his Conduct in going to Fort Wash- " ington.[1]

[1] The following are the Instructions here referred to:

POUGHKEEPSIE, Sept. 27, 1776.

" Sir—You are to proceed with your Sloop down the River as far as Mount Washington—there to take Charge of what Tackle and Apparel may be on Board the two Ships, two Brigs, and two Sloops, sent down by this Committee, intended to be sunk there, if his Excellency Genl. Washington shall think it necessary. You will carefully take the Rigging, &c., of all the Vessels on Board your Sloop, especially that belonging to the Ships, keeping it separate from the rest, or so marked that you will be able to distinguish it from what you may have on Board belonging to the other Vessels, and store the Same, on your Return, in Messrs. Schenck's Store, with the Rigging already there, belonging to the said Ships. You will also take Charge of the Boards and Plank on Board the Brig, belonging to Lothrop and others, sell them for the Market price, keep an exact

" *Refolved,* farther, That a Letter be fent to
" General Wafhington, acquainting him with our
" Proceedings.[1]

" *Refolved,* That the feveral Perfons appointed
" by this Committee for navigating the impreffed
" Veffels from hence to Fort Wafhington, do fail
" from this Place immediately to the faid Fort ;
" and all commanding Officers at the Forts and
" elfewhere on the River, in the Service of this
" State, are hereby ordered and requefted to aid

Account of the Number and Sales, and return the Amount and Monies to Capt. John Schenck to be kept for the Owner of the Boards. You are to bring the Hands back (on Board your Sloop) which we have fent to navigate the Veffels down, if they don't find an earlier Paffage—keeping Account of all your Expenfes, &c. In cafe His Excellency conceives it Needlefs to fink any or the whole of the Veffels fent down you are to have them brought back as foon as poffible, by the fame Hands that carry them down, or fuch other as you can procure. When at either of the Forts in the Highlands or at Mount Wafhington you may apply to the Commanding Officer for an Order on the Commiffary for as many Rations of Provifions as are neceffary for your Hands and thofe in the other Veffels, being all in the Continental Service."

" By Order,
" Robt. Yates, Chairman.
" To Capt. Robert North."

[1] The following is the original Draft of the Letter to Gen. Wafhington here referred to :

" Poughkeepsie, Sept. 27, 1776.

Sir—In confequence of your Excellency's Requifition, the Committee, which the Convention of this State appointed for devifing Ways and Means to obftruct the Navigation of Hudfon's River, have lately received Directions from the Convention to purchafe Veffels to be funk near Fort Wafhington. To effect this we immediately proceeded up to this Place with Capt. Grenel, whofe Affiftance, by Reafon of his naval Experience, the Convention conceived might be Ufeful to the Committee.

" The Committee, upon their Arrival here, fent down an old Sloop which we had purchafed fome Time before, and directed that another Sloop lying in the Highlands fhould alfo be fent down. Both are intended to be funk, and we make no Doubt but by this Time they are at the Bridge. As

" and affift in ballafting faid Veffels, whenever they
" fhall be called upon by any of the Skippers of the
" faid Veffels for that Purpofe.

" A Copy of the above Refolve fent to Capt.
" Henry Benfon for Ship; do, to Alexander Dean

alfo the Fire Ship charged by Capt. Hazelwood, he having charged but One here for want of Materials.

" The Committee have alfo impreffed and now fend down two large Ships and two Brigs; and in Order to afcertain their refpective Values have appointed Perfons of unexceptionable Characters and great Experience to appraife the Same on Oath, for the Purpofe that the Owners thereof may receive from the Public a Recompence. The faid Appraifement ftands as follows:

The Brig of Lothrop and others,	£400
The Brig of Malcom and others,	760
The new Ship of John Franklin,	3429
The new Ship of Samuel Franklin,	2800
	£7389
The Fire Sloop was purchafed for	200
The Sloop fent from Poughkeepfie,	125
The Sloop in the Highlands,	130
	£7844

" We found in the Brig owned by Mr. Lothrop a Quantity of Boards, and knowing they were much wanted at the Bridge, we concluded to fend them down, and have requefted Capt. North to deliver them to fuch Officer as may be appointed to receive and purchafe the fame, and at the Price ufually paid, with Power to receive the Money.

" The two Ships have never been out at Sea, and by the Report of Mafters of Veffels and Ship Carpenters they are well built and of the very beft Materials. It would, therefore, become a Matter of Concern to fink thofe Veffels, if the Intereft of the Public fhould not render the Meafure abfolutely neceffary and unavoidable.

" In order to afford Capt. Cooke proper Affiftance in procuring Plank we directed Capt. Cafewell, of the Sloop-of-War Cambden, equipped by this State, to carry down all the fpare Plank in the Ship-yards. We have alfo purchafed upwards of 6000 Feet and fent them down by Capt. Donaldfon; and as thofe Sloops proceeded down with a fair Wind on Tuefday laft we make no doubt but they are fafely arrived.

" Yr humble Servt.
" Robt. Yates, Chairman.
" To His Excellency, Genl. Wafhington."

" for the other leffer Ship ; do. to Mr. Lewes for a
" Brig ; do. to Capt. Hallock for a Brig."

The Letter from Robt. Yates, Chairman of
the Secret Committee, to the Convention,[1] fhows
that the Veffels in queftion were fent to Fort
Wafhington. The Fire Veffels fent down by
the Secret Committee do not feem to have been of
any ufe whatever. The Plank and Boards fent
down were ufed—the firft for the Conftruction of

[1] The following is the Original Draft of this Letter:

" POUGHKEEPSIE, Wednefday, 25th Sept., 1776.

" Sir : We've obtained 2 Sloops, 2 Briggs, and 2 large Ships for the Purpofe of obftructing the Channel at Fort Wafhington. One of the Sloops, the Clinton, heretofore pur-chafed by the Committee, we found here, the other we've ordered from Fort Montgomery. The two Briggs are here alfo, one of them belongs to Malcom, Kip & Lott, the other, a New England Brig about 120 tons Burthen, loaded with Wheat, Staves, and a confiderable Quantity of inch Plank—the Wheat and Staves we've ordered to be ftored, but keep the Boards for public Ufe. The Ships are in Efopus Creek, owner Meffrs. Franklin. They are two very fine Veffels, in the building of which much extraordinary Pains have been taken, both as to Timber and Work-manfhip. Upon going there we ordered them to be hauled out, and expect they will proceed to Fort Wafhington this Day. The 2 Sloops, the Clinton and that from Fort Montgomery, we think are almoft arrived at this Time, as the Clinton failed yefterday with a fair Wind and the other muft have proceeded from the Fort after the Clinton ar-rived there ; and as to the Brigs we hope we fhall be able to difpatch them to-day alfo. The Cambden, Capt. Caftle, with near 2000 Feet of Plank and Capt. Donaldfon with upwards of 6000 do. failed yefter-day alfo. The Ships and Brigs aforefaid we are to have appraifed by the Time they are ready to fet off from here ; and we imagine the Ships will run very high.

" Our Stock of Money is very low, and our Contracts and Ex-penfes far exceeding the Sum we were furnifhed with— the Demands on this Committee frequent and urgent. Upon thefe Confiderations we hope the Convention will by fome Means or other furnifh us with a farther Supply."

G

Platforms in the Fort, and the latter in completing the Bridge acrofs the Spuyten-Devil Creek. The Ships and Brigs were received by Capt. Cook.

The Minutes of the Secret Committee make no further mention of the Fort Wafhington Obftructions. As we have before remarked, the Obftructions at that Place appear to have been, entirely, under the Charge of others. From what we can gather, Tench Tilghman, Capt. Cook and the Commandant at Fort Wafhington, managed the whole Affair, receiving only the Affiftance of the Secret Committee in the Veffels fent. This is apparent from the following Letter from Tench Tilghman, dated Ocƈtober 3d, 1776 :

" Capt. Cook is now up the River cutting Tim-
" ber for the *Chevaux-de-Frize* ; as he is much
" wanted here to fink the old Veffels, the Gen.
" begs that you would immediately fend him
" down ; we are at a Stand for want of him, for as
" he has Superintended the Matter from the begin-
" ning, he beft knows the propereft places to be
" Obftrucƈted."

The hafte with which the Obftructions were completed fupplies the Inference that they were far from Perfeƈt. Indeed, they failed entirely of their Purpofe, as the Enemy's Veffels paffed them, on the 9th of Ocƈtober, without firing a Gun, as will be feen from the following Letter to the Convention :

" HEAD QUARTERS,
" Harlem Heights, 9th Oct., 1776.

" GENTLEMEN :

" About 8 o'Clock this Morning the Roebuck
" and Phœnix, and a Frigate of about 20 Guns, got
" under way from about Bloomingdale, where
" they have been laying for fome Time, and Steer-
" ed on with an eafy Southerly Breeze towards our
" *Chevaux-de-Frize,* which we hoped would have
" given them fome Interruption, while our Batte-
" ries played upon them ; but to our Surprife and
" Mortification, they all ran through without the
" leaft Difficulty, and without receiving the leaft
" apparent Damage. How far they intend to go
" up, I don't know ; but His Excellency thought
" fit to give you the earlieft Information, that you
" may put Gen. Clinton on his Guard at the
" Highlands ; for they may have Troops on Board
" to furprife thofe Forts. If you have any Stores
" on the Water fide, you had better have them re-
" moved a Second Time ;[1] Boards efpecially, for

[1] It may be proper to explain the Words, " a Second Time," here ufed. On the 12th of July, 1776, before the Obftructions at Fort Wafhington were in any confiderable State of Forwardnefs, two Britifh Veffels of War, the Phœnix and the Rofe, Sailed up the River as far as Haverftraw. Expreffes were immediately fent to the Convention informing that Body of the Fact, and to Gen. Clinton, then in Command at Fort Montgomery. Among the old Papers depofited in Wafhington's Head Quarters in Newburgh, is the following Letter to Gen. Clinton :

" HEAD QUARTERS,
" July 12th, 1776.

" SIR :

" This is juft to inform you,
" that two Men-of-War have this
" Afternoon paffed by our Forts,
" and gone up the River paft Kings

" which we fhall be put to great Straits if the
" Communication is cut off. The Enemy have
" made no Move on the Land fide.

" I am, Gent., your moft Obd't. Serv't.,

" TENCH TILGHMAN.

" Hon. Convention of New York."

This Intelligence was received with great Confternation. Surrounded by Tories, who took
courage at the Succefs of the Britifh Veffels, and

" Bridge. You will therefore take
" fuch Meafures as to put the Forts
" under your Command in the beft
" State of Defence poffible to An-
" noy the Enemy. You are alfo to
" Difpatch Expreffes along the
" River that no Veffels may fall in
" their Hands, and to give Notice
" of this Manœuvre to the Com-
" manding Officer at Albany, with
" all Expedition poffible.
" By Command of
" His Excel. Gen. Wafhington,
" I am, Sir,
" Your very Servant,
" RICH'D CAREY, Junr.,
" A. D. C.'
" P. S. I have it in Command
" farther to defire you would take
" the Carpenters from the Veffels
" which are Building at Pough-
" keepfie, and Prepare thofe Vef-
" fels which were taken from the
" Torys, and are now at Efopus,
" Kingfton, to be made ufe of as Fire
" Rafts, or to make Rafts in any
" other way Expeditioufly, that
" will Anfwer the purpofe of Har-

" raffing the Ships which are gone
" up the River,
" I am as above,
" R. CAREY, A. D. C."
" FORT CONSTITUTION,
" July 13, 1777.
" The above is a Copy of a
" Letter, I juft now Rec'd by Ex-
" prefs from the General.
" I am, Sir,
" Your Humble Servent.
" JAMES CLINTON, Col."
The Convention immediately
ordered out the Militia, and directed the Removal " of all Provi-
" fions and other Stores," both
Private and Publick Property, to
places of Safety. The Veffels,
however, made no Attempt to pafs
the Highlands, but after fupplying
the Tories with Arms and Amunition, returned to New York. No
farther Effort was made to afcend
the River until the Time of the
Paffage of the Obftructions.
The Attack of the Fire Ships on
the Rofe and Phœnix has already
been noticed. (See *ante*, p. 24.)

having to Rely only upon the half completed Fortifications in the Highlands, and the few Militia
Men who remained true to the Declaration (but
who refufed to March out of their Refpective
Counties), the Defence of the State appeared
Hopelefs and the Succefs of the Enemy Certain.
But notwithftanding the difcouraging Profpect, the
Convention determined to leave nothing undone
that could be done. An Exprefs was difpatched
to Gens. Clinton and Schuyler, then in Command
of Forts Montgomery and Clinton; the Militia
were ordered out to protect the Shores; and a
Company of Rangers was fent to Fifhkill for the
" Purpofe of detecting and fuppreffing Confpiracies
" formed in this State againft the Liberties of
" America." The following Letter, addreffed by
the Committee of Safety[1] to Gen. Wafhington
Reveals the State of Affairs:

" FISHKILL, 10th October, 1776.
" SIR:
" We received from Mr. Tilghman an account
" of the Enemy's Ships having gone up the River,
" and have Defpatched Expreffes to Gen. Schuy-
" ler and Gen. Clinton, agreeable to Your Excel-
" lency's Requeft. Nothing can be more alarming
" than the prefent Situation of our State. We are
" Daily getting the moft Authentic Intelligence of

[1] This Committee of Safety was in its behalf, during the Periods
appointed by the Convention, to act when the Latter was not in Seffion.

" Bodies of Men Enlifted and Armed, with orders
" to affift the Enemy. We much fear that thofe
" co-operating with the Enemy will feize fuch
" Paffes as will cut off all Communication between
" the Army and us, and prevent your Supplies.

" We dare not Truft any more of the Militia
" out of this County. We have called for fome
" Aid from the two adjoining ones, but beg Leave
" to fuggeft to Your Excellency the Propriety of
" fending a Body of Men to the Highlands or
" Peekfkill to fecure the Paffes, prevent Infurrec-
" tions and overaw the Difaffected.

" We fuppofe Your Excellency has taken the
" neceffary Steps to prevent the Landing of any
" Men from the Ships, fhould they be fo inclined,
" as no Reliance at all can be placed on the Militia
" of Weftchefter County."

Fortunately, however, the Veffels proceeded but
a fhort Diftance up the River; Quiet was foon
reftored, and redoubled Exertions made to complete
the Fortifications and Obftructions at Fort Montgomery.

Two Veffels only of thofe furnifhed by the Secret Committee feem to have been ufed; the
others were procured at New York. The Ships
and Brigs fent down by the Secret Committee
were evidently not ufed for that Purpofe, as will
be inferred from the following Correfpondence,
which bears Date after the Paffage of the Obftructions by the Roebuck and Phœnix, viz:

"HEAD QUARTERS, Oct. 11th, 1776.

"SIR:

"The General defires that you will Appoint "fome Perfon on behalf of the Country to take "Charge of the two Ships and two Brigs that "were fent down here to be funk.

"I am, Sir, your Humble Servant,

"WILLIAM GRAYSON, A. D. C.

"To Brig. Gen. Mifflin."

"Capt. Cook is hereby authorized to take "charge of the Ships above referred to and give a "Receipt for the Ships and Tackle.

"THOMAS MIFFLIN, B. G.

"October 11, 1776."

"Received from Capt. Henry Benfon, two "Ships and two Brigs, with the Materials herein-"after mentioned, being Veffels Ordered by the "Convention of the State of New York to this "Place for the ftopping the Channel of the North "River, oppofite to Mount Wafhington. [Here follows an Inventory of the Rigging, &c.]

"By Order of Brig. Gen. Mifflin,

"MATHEW COOK.

"Spiten-Devil Creek, 12 Oct., 1776."

We have only one more Point to note. Immediately upon the Receipt of the Intelligence of the Paffage of the Britifh Veffels up the River, the Continental Congrefs paffed an order directing

Gen. Waſhington, " by every Art and at whatever
" Expenſe, to obſtruct effectually the Navigation
" of North River, between Fort Waſhington and
" Mount Conſtitution, as well to prevent the Re-
" greſs of the Enemy's Frigates lately gone up, as
" to hinder them from receiving Succor." But
the Reduction of Fort Waſhington and the Evacuation of Fort Lee (Mount Conſtitution) followed
ſo immediately after, as to prevent any Attempt at
the Execution of this Order.

The Reduction of Fort Waſhington occurred
on the 16th of November, 1776; and was announced to the Convention of the State of New
York by Gen. Waſhington, in a Letter bearing
that Date, as follows:

" I am Sorry to inform you that this Day about
" 12 o'Clock, the Enemy made a general Attack
" upon our Lines about Fort Waſhington, which
" having carried, the Garriſon retired within the
" Fort. Col. McGraw finding there was no Proſ-
" pect of Retreating acroſs the North River, ſur-
" rendered the Poſt. We do not know our own
" loſs, or that of the Enemy in forcing the Lines,
" but I imagine it muſt have been pretty conſider-
" able on both ſides, as the Fire in ſome Parts was
" of long continuance and heavy; neither do I
" know the Terms of Capitulation. The Force of
" the Garriſon before the Attack was about 2000
" Men.   I have the Honor to be, &c.,
                              " GEO. WASHINGTON."

In a Note to his Account of the Reduction of Fort Wafhington, Loffing fays: "The Number "of Regulars was about two thoufand. There "were fix or feven hundred Militia, Volunteers "and Stragglers, all of whom were probably in- "cluded in Howe's Report of 'two thoufand fix "hundred Prifoners.' The lofs of the Americans, "in killed and wounded, did not exceed one "hundred; that of the Royal Army was almoft "one thoufand. The Heffians, as ufual, Suffered "moft feverely."

Upon obtaining Poffeffion of Fort Wafhington, the Britifh removed the Obftructions at that Place, and Demolifhed entirely Fort Lee.

H

III.

OBSTRUCTIONS

AT

FORT MONTGOMERY.

OBSTRUCTIONS

AT

FORT MONTGOMERY.

HE Obſtructions to the Naviga-
tion of the River at Fort Mont-
gomery, were conſtructed entirely by or under the Direction
of the Secret Committee. In
the Minutes of the Proceedings
of the Committee, and in the
Letters and other Documents furniſhed us in the
Clinton Papers, we have : 1ſt. The different
Plans that were propoſed, commenced and abandoned; 2d. The Plan finally adopted, and an Account of the Difficulties that attended its Execution; 3d. *The preciſe Character of the Obſtructions
when completed*; 4th. The failure that attended the

firſt Efforts to fix the Chain ; and the ſubſequent Succeſs.

Noticing theſe Points briefly, we remark, 1ſt. The Minutes ſhow that the Committee firſt agreed to Obſtruƈt the Navigation by means of a Boom, which was to be conſtruƈted in the Manner deſcribed in the following Extraƈt. " It was " Direƈted that Rafts were to be made, formed of " Pine Logs of " not leſs than " fifty feet long, " placed ten feet " apart, and framed together by three croſs Pieces ; " that each Raft be placed fifteen feet apart " and Conneƈted by ſtrong Chains of 1½ inch " Iron ; that the Rafts be anchored with their " Butts down the River ; that the Butts be " armed with Iron." (*See Minutes of July* 19*th,* *and Auguſt* 1*ſt*). In Front of the Boom thus conſtruƈted were to be placed Frames of Timber made in the following Manner : " The pointed " Beams to be of about the length of 16 feet, and " to be about 15 foot apart and two Croſs Beams " worked in and Bolted ; * * the Points or Ends " whereof to be ſhod with Iron, ſo as to Anſwer " the double purpoſe of Pounding any Veſſels that " may Sail up to it ; and if that ſhould fail, to leſ- " ſen the Shock of thoſe Veſſels when they come to " the Boom." (*See Minutes of July* 19*th*). Eſ- pecial Attention is aſked to this Deſcription, from

the Fact that it has been stated that the Chain
was placed in Front of the Boom, not only at Fort
Montgomery, but also at West Point. The fact
was exactly the reverse, and was so, not only for
the Reasons assigned by the Committee, viz: "To
"receive the first shock of those Vessels that may
"come up to it," and thus relieve the Boom or
Main Obstruction; but from the obvious Fact that
it would be a gross Absurdity to place the principal Obstruction in a Position rendering it liable to
be broken and its Purpose defeated by the first
Onset of the Enemy. Obstructions to River
Navigation should be constructed on precisely the
same Principle as is a Fortification, whose Out-
works are advanced to receive the first Assault.

2d. That the Plan of Obstructing the River by
Caissons was proposed by Gen. Philip Schuyler.

3d. That after adopting the Plan first referred
to, the Committee reconsidered their Action, and
abandoned it, resolving to construct a Chain in-
stead of a Boom. That this Plan was, in turn,
temporarily abandoned, and the Construction of
the Boom resumed. And finally, that the Boom
again gave place to the Chain; a large Portion of
the latter having been previously used in Obstructing the Navigation of the River Sorel, the Outlet
to Lake Champlain.

4th. That the Obstructions, when completed,
consisted of a *Chain floated by Spars framed to-*

gether;[1] and that *in Front of the Chain* were anchored the Frames of Timber laft defcribed in the Minutes of July 1ft.

The following Engraving, which is *copied from the original Map of the Pofition of the Chain,* found among the Papers of the Secret Committee, fhows the Manner in which it was fecured to the Shores; how it was floated on the Surface of the Water, and the Pofition of the Booms; for fo we muft

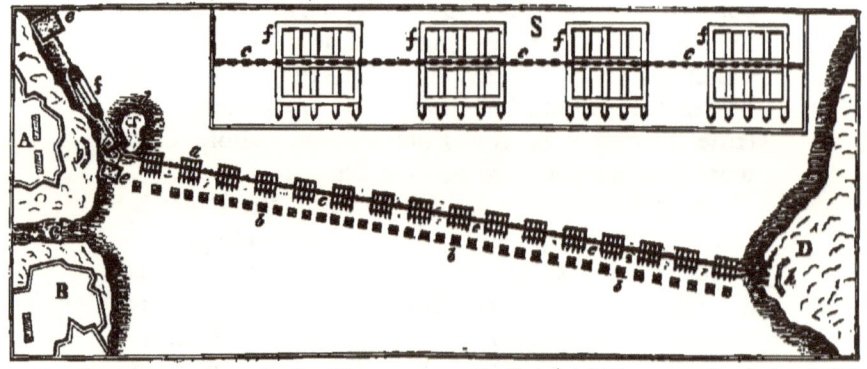

A Fort Montgomery.   B Fort Clinton.   C Poplopin's Kill.   D Anthony's Nofe.
    a Floats to Chain.   *b b b* Booms in front of Chain.   *c c c* Chain.
   d Rock at which the Chain was fecured with large Iron Roller.   *e e* Cribs and Anchors.
   f Blocks and Purchafe for tightening Chain.   *g h* Ground Batteries for defence of Chain.
        S Section fhowing Floats and Chain.   *e e e* Chain.   *f f f* Floats.

regard the Frame of Timber placed in Front of it for its Protection:

With this Explanation of the Subject, we refume the Hiftory of the Obftructions.   From the

---

[1] It is probable that a Portion of the Frames previoufly made for the Boom were ufed for this Purpofe.

Papers referred to, we learn that the Members of the Secret Committee, immediately on their Appointment, proceeded to the Highlands, for the purpofe of afcertaining the Condition of the Forts there; and to determine, by a Survey, the Character of the Obftructions neceffary, in order to clofe the River againft the Paffage of the Enemy's Veffels. The firft Meeting of the Committee was held on the 19th of July, when the following were the Proceedings:

" FORT MONTGOMERY, July 19, 1776.
" At a Meeting of the Secret Committee from the
" Convention of the State of New York: Pre-
" fent—Meffrs. Jay, Yates, R. R. Livingfton,
" G. Livingfton, and Tappan, Committee, and
" Gen. Jas. Clinton, Col. Geo. Clinton, and
" Capt. Bedlow.

" It is propofed and agreed to, that in order to
" Obftruct the Navigation of the Hudfon's River
" fo as to prevent any of the Ships of the King of
" Great Britain coming up the fame, it will be
" neceffary to throw acrofs the River at or near
" Fort Montgomery, a Boom, and below it to
" Anchor Frames of Timber, the Points or Ends
" whereof to be fhod with Iron, fo as to anfwer
" the double purpofe of Pounding any Ships that
" may Sail up to it; and if that fhould fail, to lef-
" fen the fhock of thofe Veffels when they come to
" the Boom—fuch Frames to be made in the

I

" following Manner :   The pointed
" Beams to be of about the length
" of 16 feet, and to be about 15 foot
" apart and two croſs Beams worked
" in and Bolted."

Under date of July 20th, we find the following
minutes :

" July 20th.
" Agreed to have 200 Iron Trucks caſt at the
" Furnace in the Highlands—and gave orders to
" Mr. Boyd to have Moulds made for the Pur-
" poſe.

" Alſo wrote a Letter to General Waſhington,
" appriſing him of our Proceedings and requeſting
" him to ſend to the Forts in the Highlands a
" number of Artillery Men.[1]

[1] The Following is the original Draft of this Letter :

" FORT WASHINGTON,
20 July, 1776.

SIR—We informed your Excellency of our Appointment, and in Conſequence of which we took a Survey of the Fortreſs in the Highlands. We are extremely ſorry to ſay, that notwithſtanding their Importance and advantageous Situation, they are by no Means in a proper Poſture of Defence. Part of the few Cannon at Fort Conſtitution were ſent away, and the whole Number now there and at Fort Montgomery are not ſufficient. This Want we ſuppoſe your Excel-lency will be unable to Supply. We have therefore ſent for thoſe that were deſigned for the Ships that are building at Poughkeepſie ; but if we ſhould obtain them they will be of little Uſe unleſs ſome *Matroſſes* can be ſpared from New York ſince there are only 14 at both Forts. If your Excellency could ſpare a few Howitzers they might be of ſignal Uſe at this Place. A ſkillful Engineer would be at no Place more Serviceable than here, as many ſmall Poſts which command this ought to be Fortified. We cannot think the Garriſons by any Means proportioned to the Extent of the Works or the Importance of

" Alfo, wrote a Letter to the Proprietors of the
" Iron Furnace at Salifbury requefting them to
" fend to the landing of Col. Hoffman, all 20 of
" the heavy Cannon they may have caft, for the
" ufe of the Shipping at Poughkeepfie.
" Alfo, wrote a Letter to the Convention ap-
" prifing them of our Proceedings."[1]
The next Meeting of the Committee was held

the Place. We know the Difficulty that your Excellency will find in fupplying thefe Wants, yet we can not but fuggeft them, fince we are fatiffied that even if the Enemy fhould be Defeated at New York they may yet take fuch Pofts here as we fhould find it Impoffible to Difpoffefs them of.

" Since writing the Above we have been informed that the Salifbury Furnace, at which Place the Cannon are caft, is under the Direction of the Government of Connecticut, fo that we have fome Doubt whether we can procure thofe for which we wrote unlefs your Excellency be pleafed to lend us your Affiftance by writing to Gov. Trumbel on the Subject.

Robt. Yates, Chn. of Com.

[1] The following is the Draft of the Letter to the Convention:

" Fort Montgomery,
" July 21, 1776.

" Gentln.—In Confequence of a late Refolution of the Convention of this State we are appointed a Secret Committee to devife Ways and Means for obftructing the Channel of Hudfon's River. We have determined to throw a Boom acrofs the River in order to prevent the Enemy's Ships from paffing the Forts in the Highlands, and for this Purpofe we fhall want 150 White Pine Logs, or any other Wood that will float, of the Length of 14 feet.[1] You will, therefore, pleafe to procure them, and fend them to Poughkeepfie to Meffrs. Van Zandt, Tudor and Lawrence with the utmoft Difpatch. As two Ships are already advanced as far as Haverftraw, and only wait for a favorable Opportunity to pafs the Fortifications, the Neceffity of a Boom is rendered exceedingly preffing. We truft, therefore, that you will exert yourfelves upon this Occafion and fend the Logs as faft as they can be procured. You will be immediately furnifhed with Monie by one of our monied Members who leaves this Place for Albany to-morrow.

" We are, Gentlemen, &c."

[1] Thefe Logs were fubfequently rafted to New Windfor and ufed in conftructing the Boom at Weft Point.

July 25th, 1776.   The following were the Proceedings:

"POUGHKEEPSIE, July 25th, 1776.
" Preſent—The Committee as before.
" It is Propoſed and Agreed to, that a Boom be
" drawn acroſs the Hudſon's River at the High-
" lands.   That an Expreſs be ſent Gen. Schuyler[1]

---

[1] The following is the original Draft of the Letter to Gen. Schuyler. It is without date—as follows:
" SIR—The encloſed Copy of ſome late Reſolutions of the Convention of the State of New York will inform you, that we are a Committee of that Body and charged with the Execution of the Buſineſs mentioned in them.

" As the Chain intended to Obſtruct the River Sorel cannot now be applied to that Uſe, and will Serve to prevent the Enemy's Ships from going beyond the Hook on Hudſon's River, we muſt beg the Favor of you to ſend it (the whole or ſuch Parts of it as may expeditiouſly be had) to Poughkeepſie, and Conſigned to Meſſrs. Van Zante, Lawrence and Tudor, with the utmoſt Diſpatch.

" Be pleaſed to inform thoſe Gentlemen of the length of ſuch Part of the Chain as you can ſend, in order that they may direct the defficiency to be Supplied.

" We ſhall, by this Opportunity, requeſt of the Committee of Albany immediately to furniſh us with 150 ſaw Logs of the largeſt ſize to ſupport the Chain; and we flatter ourſelves that your Attention and Influence will be extended to both theſe Objects.

" We have the honor be, Sir, with the greateſt eſteem and reſpect,

" Your moſt obedient
" And hble. ſervt."

To this Letter, Gen. Schuyler ſent the following Reply:

" GERMAN FLATS,
" July 25th, 1776.

" GENTLEMEN—Your Letter of the 20th Inſt., from Poughkeepſie, was delivered to me at nine this Morning. I have tranſmitted a Copy of it, and of the Reſolution it incloſed, to General Gates, with directions to ſend the Chain to you, under the Charge of a careful Officer, *if it can be ſpared*. Before I left Tyconderoga, we had it in Contemplation to Draw it acroſs that Part of Lake Champlain which Divides Tyconderoga from the Camp we occupy on the Eaſt Shore oppoſite to it. I would not wiſh you, therefore to make too great a dependence upon receiving it. If it cannot be ſpared, Meſſrs. Van

" for the Chain intended to be thrown acrofs the
" River Sorrel, to be employed for the above pur-
" pofe; and as it may fall fhort of the Diftance
" required, it is farther concluded to Apply to Col.
" R. Livingfton to make until countermanded by
" this Committee, a quantity of Bar-Iron of about
" 1½ inches fquare, and to be fent from Time to
" Time to the Works at Poughkeepfie."

On the Margin of the Minutes of this Meeting
is the following Memoranda :

Zant, Lawrence and Tudor will be Advized of it without delay.

" Whether the Chain is fent or not, you may ftand in need of the faw Logs. For perhaps, you will think it Expedient, if the Chain cannot be procured, to fink Cafoons or Sloops filled with Stone and funk in the River from *Tan-canten-book* to the Eaftern Shore, to ftop the Paffage. Part of the Channel there is fo fhallow that I was once on Board of a Sloop deeply laden which touched at low Water. And that in any part where the Channel there is too deep, two Caffoons or Veffels, one upon the other, would anfwer the Purpofe. A Paffage might be left open in the fhalloweft part, and one or more Veffels ready for finking kept at Hand. This Place is indeed above Fort Montgomery, but the Enemy would find it extremely Difficult to Force a Paffage through the High-lands if a Body of Troops well in-trenched were oppofed to them at the narrow Paffage juft beyond the firft Houfe in the Highlands, and between that and where Teller formerly lived. This may have occurred to you; and perhaps there are Difficulties which I am unac-quainted. I have ventured to men-tion this, well knowing that my Motives will be a fufficient Apology with you for the Liberty I have taken in doing fo.

" I am, Gentlemen,
   " Your moft obedt.
      " And humbl. Servt.,
         " PH. SCHUYLER."

" To ROBT. YATES, Efq., Chair-man, and the reft of the Gentle-men of the Secret Committee, &c."

This Reply to Gen. Schuyler is a curious Affair. The Suggeftions which he makes evidently refer to the finking of Caffoons near Pollo-pel's Ifland—but we have been un-able to locate Tancanten Hook.

"For 600 yds., or 1800 feet of Chain, you " want 4800 foot of Bar Iron in length."

At this Meeting Artizans were appointed to conftruƈt the Works agreed upon; and the follow-- ing Inftruƈtions iffued to them:

" The Convention of the State of New York, " having, by a Refolution of the 16th Day of July " Inftant appointed us a Committee, among other " things to devife Means for Fortifying Hudfon's " River, and Obftruƈting its Navigation; and for " carrying the fame into Execution, we have " thought it neceffary to appoint, and do hereby " appoint Jacobus Van Zante, Auguftus Lawrence " and Samuel Tudor, or any two of them, to " Superintend the following Work (under the Di- " reƈtion of fuch of the Members of this Com- " mittee as may remain or be at Poughkeepfie):

" 1ft. The making of a Chain to fix acrofs " Hudfon's River at the moft convenient place " near Fort Montgomery, and fixing the fame; " and if it fhould be found Impraƈticable at or near " the faid Fort, then to fix the fame at or near Fort " Conftitution.   *   *   *   *   *

" If it fhould happen that none of this Com- " mittee fhould be at Poughkeepfie, in that cafe " the faid Van Zandt, Lawrence and Tudor are " direƈted to inform the Chairmain of this Com- " mittee, or any of the Members, of the Meafures " they have taken in confequence of this appoint-

" ment. And we hereby engage, for and in be-
" half of the State of New York, to Defray the
" Expenſe attending the Execution of this Work,
" as well as to make to the ſaid Van Zandt, Law-
" rence and Tudor a reaſonable allowance for their
" trouble."

By theſe Inſtructions, it will be ſeen that the
original Deſign was changed. Inſtead of a *Boom*,
the Artizans named were directed to make and
" fix a *Chain* acroſs the Hudſon's River," &c.

And here we remark, that the Diſtinction made
by the Secret Committee, between a Boom and a
Chain, ſhould be particularly obſerved. In many
Inſtances, and eſpecially in Engliſh Hiſtories, the
whole Obſtruction was ſpoken of as a Boom, not
only in reference to that at Fort Montgomery but
alſo that at Weſt Point. Strictly ſpeaking, this
would, perhaps, be a correct Deſignation ; but the
Secret Committee applied the terms *Boom* and
Chain to ſpecify different Parts of the Work, inſtead
of employing them convertibly. This Diſtinction
was obſerved, not only in the Fort Montgomery
Obſtructions, but alſo in conſtructing thoſe at Weſt
Point ; and in this Senſe we uſe the terms—that is,
as ſpecifying ſeparate Parts of the Obſtructions.
Hence we have ſaid that there was a Boom and a
Chain at Fort Montgomery, and a Boom and a
Chain at Weſt Point, when the Obſtructions at
thoſe Points were ſeverally completed.

A Meeting of the Committee was held at Albany, July 27, 1776, but the Minutes are entirely illegible. The next Meeting of the Committee was held on the 1ſt Aug., 1776 — Preſent, G. Livingſton, Robert R. Livingſton, and William Paulding. At this Meeting the Committee ſeem to have regarded it as impoſſible to get the Chain conſtructed in Time to be of any Service, and paſſed a Reſolution returning to the Plan adopted at their firſt Meeting (July 16), as will be ſeen from the following :

"*Reſolved,* That it appears to the Members of
" this Committee, that the Chain intended for the
" River Sorel, will, in all probability, be retained at
" Ticonderoga; that the making one of ſufficient
" Length will occaſion great Delay; that the Rafts
" heretofore agreed upon by this Committee, at
" the Meeting held at Fort Montgomery, and laid
" aſide on Account of the Difficulty of procuring
" the neceſſary Spars, will be the moſt effectual and
" ſpeedy Means of obſtructing the Navigation of
" the River; that it appears to this Committee,
" that the Wood neceſſary for forming the Rafts
" may be procured, a Contract having been made
" for the ſame by Mr. Tappen, with the Approba-
" tion of Robt. Yates, Eſq., and Mr. R. Livingſton.

[1] The following is the Contract here referred to :

" (Copy.) I agree to the pro-
" poſals made to me by Mr. White

" and ſignified by Letter of Mr. R.
" Livingſton, reſpecting the Deli-
" very of 160 Spars of 50 (feet)
" long in Hudſon's River on the

" *Refolved*, Therefore, that Mr. Jacobus Van
" Zandt, Mr. Lawrence and Mr. Tudor be direct-
" ed to form the Rafts agreeable to the following
" Plan : That each Raft be formed of five Logs
" of not lefs than fifty feet in length, placed ten
" feet apart, and framed together by three crofs
" Pieces ; that each Raft be placed fifteen feet
" apart and Connected by ftrong Chains of 1½
" inch thick, and anchored with their Butts down
" the River ; that the Butts be fhod with iron.

" That each Member of this Committee be
" directed to Enquire for and Purchafe as many

" laft Day of next Week ; for
" which, if Mr. Robt. R. Living-
" fton and Robt. Yates agree to, I
" think they reafonably deferve the
" Sum of £1000.
          " Signed,
                    " CHRISTOPHER TAPPEN.
     " July 26th, 1776."
     The following is the Bill for thefe
Logs :
               " POUGHKEEPSIE, }
          " Sept. 15th, 1776. }
" The Honorable Convention of
     " the State of New York.
" To John R. Livingfton & White,
                              Dr.
     " For 160 large Trees, as per
" Contract made with your Secret
" Convention,..........£1000"
     Here is another Bill for Logs—
which feem to be thofe referred to
in the Letter to the Convention
(note 2) and by Gen. Schuyler in
his Letter to the Committee, viz :

" The Committee of the Con-
" vention of the State of New York.
" To Robt. Van Rensselaer, Dr.
" To 111 Pieces of Timber of 45
     " feet and upwards in length, at
     " 50 per Piece,... £277   0   0
" To 55 Trees cut and
     " by agreement with
     " the Proprietors I
     " was to Pay at the
     " Rate of 40s per
     " Tree, but before
     " the removal there-
     " of   my   Orders
     " were   counter-
     " manded,.......   11   0   0
" To rafting the Tim-
     " ber from Outh-
     " out's to Albany,.   7   0   0
                              ─────────
                              £275 10   0
" Albany, Augft 5th, 1776.
     " Received of Robt. Yates on
     act. £114 10 0."

K

" Anchors and Cables as they can procure and
" fend Word to this Committee by the 7th Day
" of this Month of the Number they can obtain.

" *Refolved*, That it appears to this Committee
" that Robt. R. Livingfton ought to go down to
" New York and remain with the General in order
" to give him all the Affiftance in his Power in
" forwarding fuch Operations as His Excellency
" may have formed for the Defence of this State;
" and that for that Purpofe Mr. Livingfton be
" vefted with all the Powers of this Committee fo
" far as he may deem it neceffary to exert the
" fame.

" In cafe it fhall appear to Mr. Livingfton un-
" neceffary for him to remain in New York, that
" he can return to this place."

It does not appear, however, that this Plan was
carried out, farther than by procuring the neceffary Logs, as the Conftruction of the Chain was ftill
continued and was evidently fubfequently placed
acrofs the River. The 1½ inch Iron ordered for
the Chains mentioned in the Refolutions was
Worked up into Chain to ftrengthen the large
Chain (*Minutes Oct.* 9); and of the Logs, a Part
was probably ufed for the Floats to the Chain, and
another Part rafted to New-Windfor for the
Chevaux-de-Frize at Pollopel's Ifland.

The next Meeting of the Convention was held
on the 13th Auguft, of which the following are
the Minutes:

" Poughkeepfie. At a Meeting of the Secret Com-
" mittee of the Convention of New York, Aug.
" 13th, 1776. Prefent—Robt. Yates, Chn.,
" John Jay, Gilbert Livingfton, Chrift. Tappen.
" Read a Letter from Gen. Wafhington of the
" 21ft ult. Mr. Jay delivered in a Report of his
" Proceedings in Connecticut and elfewhere, which
" was read and approved of.[1] Mr. Jay, according
" to Order, alfo produced a Draft of a Letter to his
" Excellency Gen. Wafhington, which was read
" and approved of, and ordered to be engroffed.[2]
" Alfo, a Draft of another Letter to the Conven-
" tion of New York, which was alfo read and ap-
" proved of, and ordered to be engroffed.

" The Smiths, to wit: Meffrs. George Smart,
" Ifaac Van Duzen, Theop. Anthony and James
" Odill waited on the Committee in order to in-
" form them at what Rate they would undertake
" to make Bolts for the Floats to the Chain. They
" offered to make them at the Rate of 32s per
" cwt.

" *Refolved,* That there be allowed to Mr. Ifaac
' Sheldon the Sum of twenty-five dollars for his
" Services in going up to Albany and affifting the
" Committee in procuring the Materials for the

[1] This Document is among the Clinton Papers with the neceffary Paffes for its tranfmiffion to Albany. Why it was never forwarded is a Myftery. It refers mainly to pro- curing Cannon, &c., for the Forts in the Highlands.

[2] This Letter to Gen. Wafhing- ton was for a Supply of Powder for armed Veffels.

" Defenfe of Hudfon's River, and attending at
" Poughkeepfie from the 23d of July laft to the
" prefent Day.   And ordered that Mr. G. Living-
" fton Pay him or his Order the above Sum.

" Received a Letter from R. Livingfton to John
" Jay, Efq., dated the 12th Aug., 1776, acquaint-
" ing him that he cannot complete the Trucks for
" want of proper Hands to Mould them.   Alfo,
" received another Letter from the fame Perfon,
" dated the 11th Inft., directed to G. Livingfton,
" acquainting him that 2 tons of Iron was carried
" down to his Landing, and that three tons would
" be ready on Tuefday next, and on Saturday next
" 5 tons more, and requefts him to fend a Veffel
" for it.

" P. M.   *Refolved*, That the Meffrs. G. Living-
" fton and Chriftopher Tappen pay into the Hands
" of the Commiffioners and Superintendents of the
" Ship-Yards at Poughkeepfie the Sum of three
" hundred pounds, on Account of Expenfes in-
" curred or to be incurred by the Execution of the
" Orders which they have or may receive from this
" Committee.

" Agreed to give an order in favor of Dirk
" Schuyler for £15 for bringing the *Chain* and
" fome Pine Knots from Albany."

The only point of fpecial Intereft in thefe Proceedings is that in reference to bringing the *Chain*
down from Albany.   This Chain muft have been

that intended for the River Sorel, for which application had been made to Gen. Schuyler. The next Meeting was held Aug. 14th, and was confined to making Arrangements for Supplies of Provifions, Powder, Men, &c., for the Veffels of War fitting out at Poughkeepfie. The following Refolution was paffed.

" It being neceffary that Meffrs. Yates and Jay " fhould for fome Time be abfent from the Com- " mittee,

" *Refolved*, That fuch of the Members lefs than " a Quorum as may be prefent at Poughkeepfie, " have power to Execute all the Refolutions of this " Committee which they have already made ; that " they confult with Capt. Hazelwood on the beft " Means of fixing the Chain, and caufe it to be " done in fuch Manner as to them fhall appear " beft calculated to Anfwer the purpofe it is de- " figned for."

The Minutes of the Meetings held on the 22d, 23d, 25th and 27th of September we have given in connection with the Obftructions at Fort Wafhington, to which they refer. At the Meeting of the 27th September, however, vigorous Efforts feem to have been made to complete the Chain, as appears from the following Refolutions :

" *Refolved*, That the feveral Blackfmiths em- " ployed in the Continental Service in the Ship

" Yards at Poughkeepfie, (purfuant to a Refolve
" of the Congrefs at Philadelphia), be ordered and
" requefted, and they are hereby ordered and re-
" quefted, to proceed with all poffible Expedition
" in making and completing the Chain which has
" been ordered to be made by this Committee, and
" that they feverally defift from any other Bufinefs
" until they have completed the faid Chain as foon
" as furnifhed with Iron.

" *Refolved*, That Meffrs. Smart, Van Deufen,
" Anthony and Odel, or either of them are hereby
" impowered to imprefs Wagons and Teams to
" draw Coal, paying the ufual Price of the Country;
" likewife, to imprefs Coal at the ufual Price for
" Coal; they paying for the fame; that the Public
" Bufinefs may not be retarded.

" *Refolved*, That Gilbert Livingfton pay Meffrs.
" Franklin & Spifford one hundred and twelve
" pounds fifteen fhillings for two Hogfheads of
" Rum purchafed of them by this Committee."[1]

The next Meeting of the Committee was held
Oct. 9th. The following are the Minutes:

[1] The following is the Bill of
Franklin & Spifford;
" POCEPSEY, 27th Septmr. 1776.
" The Secrit Committy of the Convention of N. York,
   Bot. of Franklin & Spifford.
   2 Hhds Weft india Rum.
   113—12
   110— 6
   ————223 18

223 18
18
——————
205 Gls. at 11s. £112 15

We fhall fee, prefently, the Ufe
which was made of this Rum.
That it was not for " Medicinal
Purpofes," will be inferred.

" In Secret Committee, the 9th of Oct., 1776.
" Prefent—Gilbert Livingfton, Robert Harper,
" Jacob Cuyler, Robt. R. Livingfton.

" *Refolved,* That the inch-and-a-half Iron at
" Poughkeepfie be worked up into Chain in order
" to ftrengthen the large Chain.

" *Refolved,* That a Fortification be erected at
" Weft Point in order to Defend the Chain, and
" that Robt. Harper, Henry Wifner, Jacob Cuyler
" and Gilbert Livingfton be a Committee to carry
" the faid Refolve into execution.

" *Refolved,* That the faid Gentlemen erect any
" other Work that they may deem neceffary for
" the Defence of the Chain ; or the fecurity of
" Anthony's Nofe, which commands Fort Mont-
" gomery.

" *Refolved,* That a Letter be written to the Hon.
" the Congrefs praying Leave to employ the Car-
" penters now at Work upon the Ships building
" at Poughkeepfie, and that Robt. R. Livingfton
" draft the Letter."

The laft Meeting of the Committee, of which
we have the Minutes, was held Oct. 14, 1776.
At this Meeting we have the name of Mr. Machin[1]

[1] THOMAS MACHIN was born in Staffordfhire, England, 20th March, 1744 ; was employed by Brindley in conftructing the Canal of the Duke of Bridgewater ; afterwards made a Voyage to the Eaft Indies, and in 1772 came to America, for the purpofe of examining a Copper Mine in New Jerfey. He after-wards took up his Refidence in Bofton, and efpoufing the popular Feeling of the Time, made one of the Tea Party in 1773 ; was wounded at Bunker Hill, while act-

firſt mentioned, but not in connection with the conſtruction of the Chain, he having been previouſly employed in completing the Forts. He was directed to conſtruct Batteries. The following were the Proceedings:

ing as Lieut. of Artillery; 18th Jan., 1776, was commiſſioned 2d Lieut. of Artillery in Col. Knox's Regiment, and was employed from April to June in that Year in laying out the Fortifications for the Defence of the Town and Harbour of Boſton; 21ſt July, 1776, was directed by Waſhington to proceed to the Highlands on the Hudſon River to Act as Engineer under Col. Geo. Clinton, and there continued ſeveral Years, in conſtructing the Fortifications which the Government undertook for the Purpoſe of rendering the River impaſſable to Britiſh Veſſels. In October, 1777, when Forts Montgomery and Clinton, were taken by the Britiſh, Capt. Machin was wounded by a Muſket Ball, which entered his Breaſt and paſſed out under his right Shoulder. On his Recovery, he was again actively engaged in repairing the Damages which the Britiſh had done to the Forts, and in throwing Booms and other Obſtructions acroſs the River. In April, 1779, he accompanied Col. Van Schaick's Expedition againſt the Onondagas, of which he kept a Journal; in May of the ſame Year he ſurveyed the Water Level between Albany and Schenectady, with a View to the Supply of Albany with Water; and in June joined Sullivan's Expedition to the Geneſee Valley, as Engineer. A Map of this Expedition, executed by him, is in the poſſeſſion of his Son, Capt. Thomas Machin. In the Fall of 1781, he aided in laying out the Works of the American Army then beſieging Yorktown. In Auguſt, 1782, he married Suſan Daughter of James Van Noſtrand, of Huntington, L. I. In 1783, he began a Settlement at New Grange, Ulſter County, and in the following Year erected ſeveral Mills at the Great Pond, a few Miles Weſt of Newburgh. In 1787 he formed one of a Company for the Coinage of Copper, which does not ſeem to have been proſperous. March 12th, 1793, he was Commiſſioned a Captain, to take Rank as ſuch from 21ſt Aug., 1780. In January, 1797, he removed to the Town of Mohawk, in Montgomery County, N. Y., where he practiſed Surveying, and where he died, at his Reſidence in Charleſton, a Part of the old Town of Mohawk, 3d April, 1819, aged 72. (Simms's *Hiſtory of Schoharie County*).

" FORT CONSTITUTION, Oct. 14th, 1776.
" Prefent—Mr. Harper, Mr. Cuyler, Mr. G. Liv-
" ingfton, Gen. J. Clinton, Col. Bailey, Mr.
" Machin, Engineer.

" Confidering that there are no Works erected
" at this Poft that can defend the Chain propofed
" to be ftretched acrofs the River here, and the
" impracticability of executing any in Seafon for
" the above purpofe, and believing that the River
" at Fort Montgomery in the narroweft place is
" but 1600 feet wide, which exceeds the width of
" the River here but 100 feet, therefore,

" *Refolved,* That Mr. Machin immediately pre-
" pare a place on each Side the River at Fort
" Montgomery to faften the Ends of the intended
" Chain to; that he place two or three Guns in a
" fmall Breaft-work to be erected for that purpofe
" on the Flat place juft under the North end of the
" Grand Battery, where the Fire-Rafts now lay;
" alfo a fmall work, if Time permit, near the
" Water Edge, on the South fide of Poplopen's
" Kill."

On the Back of thefe Minutes is an Outline
Map of the Pofition of the Chain, the Forts and
the Batteries erected and to be erected. The Pofition of the Ground Batteries will be feen (*g h*) on
the Map.[1] The precife Time at which the Chain
was placed acrofs the River is not fhown, By the

---

[1] *Ante* p. 64.

Minutes laſt given it is apparent that it was then nearly ready ; and we immediately after find the following Refolution paſſed by the Convention, on the 22d Oĉtober, viz :

" *Reſolved,* That Mr. Gilbert Livingſton, one of " the Secret Committee, be direĉted to fend down " to Fort Montgomery ſuch parts of the Chain as " is fixed to the Logs ; and that Mr. Henry Wiſner, " Jr., coöperate with him in carrying this Meaſure " into Execution in the moſt Safe and Expeditiouṣ " Manner poſſible."

The next Intimation which we have of it is in a Letter addreſſed by the Preſident of the Convention to John Hancock, Preſident of the Continental Congreſs, ſtating that the Chain had broken twice. From theſe two Dates it is evident that the Chain muſt have been firſt placed acroſs the River in the early part of November. The Letter laſt referred to, ſays :

" The great length of the Chain, being upwards " of 1800 feet, the Bulk of the Logs which was " neceſſary to ſupport it, the immenſe weight of " the Water which it accumulated, have baffled " all our Efforts. It feparated twice after holding " only a few Hours."[1]

[1] Upon receiving Notice of the breaking of the Chain, the Convention, on the 23d Nov., direĉted the Secret Committee to refuſe Payment to the Smiths who made it. The following is the Refolution :

" *Reſolved,* That the Committee " appointed to Obſtruĉt the Navi- " gation of Hudſon's River, be in-

The breaking of the Chain feems to have been a Difficulty not apprehended by thofe engaged in its Conftruction, and upon the Occurrence of that Event, confiderable doubt was expreffed as to the Succefs of any Effort to Obftruct the Navigation with a Chain. A Conference was called in reference to the Subject at which Tench Tilghman, Robt. Yates, Gen. Heath and Gen. Schuyler gave their Views as to the beft Mode of fixing and fupporting the Chain. Gen. Schuyler's fuggeftions were fubmitted by Letter as follows: "A Chain "fufficiently long to reach acrofs the River ought "to have better fupporters than floating Logs; "perhaps Caffoons from thirty to forty feet

"ftructed not to Pay the Black- "fmiths who made the Chain "which was lately drawn acrofs "faid River, and broken by the "Tide, until fuch Time as the "fufficiency of their Work can be "properly Examined; and that "faid Committee take proper "Meafures for that Purpofe."

The Secret Committee immediately appointed a Commiffion to Examine the Workmanfhip of the Chain, who reported as follows:

"FORT MONTGOMERY,
"December 9, 1776.

"Thefe are to Certify that "the Chain that has been ftretched "acrofs the North River, at this "Poft, has been broken twice; the "firft, a Swivel broke, which came "from Ticonderogo, which was

"not welded Sound; the fecond "Time, a Clevin broke, which was "made at Poughkeepfie, in a folid "Part of the Chain, and no flaw "to be feen in any Part of faid "Chain. Which we do Certify "at the requeft of Meffrs. Odle "and Vanduzer.

"JAMES CLINTON, B. G.
"ABM SWARTWOUT, Captain,
"JAS. ROSECRANS, Captain,
"DANIEL LAWRENCE, Lieut."

On receiving this Report the Convention, on the 12th Dec.,

"*Refolved*, That the Committee "to Obftruct the Navigation of the "Hudfon River, be directed to pay "the Blackfmiths who made the "Chain which was lately drawn "acrofs faid River, according to "their agreement with them."

"ſquare * * * might anſwer the end. If
" twenty-five ſuch Caſſoons were ſunk at nearly
" equal diſtances, the intermediate ſpace between
" each would be about two hundred feet. The
" tops of the Caſſoons might come up to within
" two feet of the ſurface of the Water at ebb Tide,
" and the Chain run through them." This Suggeſtion was conſidered impracticable from the
depth of the Water (80 feet). Mr. Machin, the
Engineer engaged in the Erection of the Forts,
was preſent at the Conſultation and ſuggeſted that,
" with proper alterations" the Chain might ſtill be
made uſeful; and on the 30th Nov., 1776, the
Committee paſſed the following Reſolution, viz:

" *Reſolved*, That Mr. Machin, the Engineer be
" requeſted and authorized to alter and fix the
" Chain intended for the Obſtruction of the Hud-
" ſon's River, &c."

We do not find anything ſhowing the preciſe
Nature of the alterations propoſed by Mr. Machin.
Sparks in his *Life of Waſhington*, intimates that
they conſiſted in placing the Chain *under* the
Floats, inſtead of over them. However, this may
be, it is evident that the alterations were in the
Floats, and not in the Chain. Whatever they
were, they were immediately commenced and
proſecuted with Vigor. The Work was removed
to New Windſor—where the *Chevaux-de-Frize* for
the Pollopel's Iſland Obſtructions were being pre-

pared—and conducted under the Supervifion of Gov. Clinton. On the 7th March, 1777, a Committee was directed to vifit the Fortifications in the Highlands and report on the Progrefs of the Obftructions. This Committee reported that the Work was in a " great forwardnefs"—" the Tim-" ber for buoying the Chain prepared," &c. In a Letter from Gov. Clinton, dated New Windfor, March 14th, 1777, he fays:

" We only wait now for Anchors and Cables to " draw the Chain acrofs the River; the Logs for " buoying it are all completely fixed, and are this " Day fent off in a Raft down the River."

On the 23d March, he writes:

" A number of our Hands were fent down to " Fort Montgomery Yefterday, to prepare for " drawing the Chain acrofs the River," &c.

No farther Difficulty occurred with the Chain, and it continued in good Order up to the Time of its Removal by the Britifh.

The Expedition under Vaughan and Wallace paffed up the River on the 4th of October, 1777, and attacked and reduced Forts Clinton and Montgomery on the 7th of that Month. At the Time of the Attack the Forts were not half Garrifoned. Many of the Men were off to their Farms, engaged in getting in their Winter Grain ; and, in Addition to this, Gen. Putnam, miftaking

the Point of Attack, had taken fome twelve hundred Men for the Relief of Fort Independence and
Peekfkill Landing. The noife of the Confliƈt at
Fort Montgomery made him aware of his Error,
and he haftened back. Before he arrived, however, the Enemy had poffeffed themfelves of the
Forts. The Americans made a moft gallant Defence. " Never," fays Gen. Putnam in his Report
to Gen. Wafhington, " did Men behave with more
" Spirit and Aƈtivity than our Troops upon this
" occafion. They repulfed the Enemy three
" Times, who where in number at leaft five to
" one." The Enemy deftroyed Forts Montgomery
and Conftitution and the Obftruƈtions in the River.
Fort Clinton was Repaired and occupied by them,
and its Name changed to Fort *Vaughan*. Their
Occupation lafted twenty Days, when, on the return of the Expedition, this Fort was alfo deftroyed, and the Enemy retreated to New York, fmart-
ing under the Defeat of Burgoyne at Saratoga.

Loffing, in his *Field-Book*, drops the Cur-
tain over the Obftruƈtions as follows :

" Above the Boom, the Americans had two
" Frigates, two Galleys and an armed Sloop. On
" the fall of the Forts, the Crews of thefe Veffels
" fpread their Sails, and flipping their Cables, at-
" tempted to efcape up the River, but the Wind
" was adverfe and they were obliged to abandon
" them. They fet them on Fire, when they left,, to

" prevent their falling into the Hands of the Ene-
" my. The Flames fuddenly broke forth, and, as
" every Sail was fet, the Veffels foon became mag-
" nificent Pyramids of Fire. The Reflection on
" the fteep Face of the oppofite Mountains, and
" the long train of ruddy Light which fhone upon
" the Water for a prodigious diftance had a won-
" derful Effect; while the Ear was awfully filled
" with the continued Echoes from the rocky fhores
" as the Flames reached the loaded Cannons. The
" whole was fublimely terminated by the Explo-
" fions, which left all again in Darknefs. Early in
" the Morning, the Obftructions in the River,
" which had coft the Americans a quarter million
" of Dollars, Provincial Money, were deftroyed by
" the Britifh Fleet."[1]

Thus it will be feen that the Obftructions at
Fort Montgomery failed in their Purpofe. The
Chain and Booms, and the armed Ships and Brigs,
were alike without Avail—the Forts were the Key
to the River, and thefe reduced, the Paffage was
at once unlocked.

A mafs of Correfpondence, in refpect to the

[1] The exact Coft of the Obftructions cannot now be afcertained,
but were eftimated at £70,000
fterling. The Chain was of moft
excellent Workmanfhip. It was
taken up by the Britifh and fent to
England, and thence to Gibralter,
where it was of great Ufe in protecting the Shipping at the Moles.

*(Beatfon's Naval and Mil. Me-
moirs,* IV, 236). Another Boom
near Fort Conftitution, which muft
likewife have Coft much Money
and Labour, was rendered Ufelefs.
(Ib.) A large Portion of the
Chain was from Fort Ticonderoga,
and the Remainder manufactured
at Poughkeepfie.

Operations of the Secret Committee, is preſerved, from which we cull a few ſpicy Specimens.   Under Date of Sept. 11, 1776, the Convention addreſſed to the Committee the following Letter:

"FISHKILL, Sept. 11, 1776.

"SIR: It is conceived highly neceſſary that the "Iron Chain ſhould be immediately diſpatched. "If it is finiſhed, pray ſend it down to the Fort "without Delay.   If it is not finiſhed let no Time "be loſt, and in the Interim give us the earlieſt "particular Account of its preſent State and when "it will probably be finiſhed.

"I am, Sir, your very humble Servt.,

"ABM. YATES, Pres.

"To Gilbert Livingſton, Eſq., Poughkeepſie."

Gilbert Livingſton replied to this Letter in the following ſatisfaɛtory Manner:

"POUGHKEEPSIE, Sept. 14th, 1776.

"SIR: Your Letter of the 11th current is ſafely "came to Hand.   Am ſorry it is not in my Power "to take the Chain down to the Fort.   The Iron "the Committee (by the advice of the Smiths) "firſt engaged, on Working up we find vaſtly "ſhort of the Quantity wanted.   Since I have been "here, have been obliged (no other Member of "the Committee being with me) to ſend an Ex- "preſs to the Forge for ten tun more.   This, I "fear, will cauſe a Delay we by no Means expeɛt- "ed, and as finiſhing the Work depends on the

" Contingency of getting the Iron, it is impoffible
" for me to give the Time when it will be finifhed.
" I fincerely wifh that at leaft one of the Gentle-
" men of the Committee were with me, as I ex-
" pect to be obliged to go down to the Fort, to
" fee that the Aparatus is got ready to faften and
" ftretch the Chain with, that there may be no
" delay on that account. If one of the Gentlemen
" comes up, it will be neceffary that he bring at
" leaft two or three thoufand Pounds with him, as
" our Treafury is nearly exhaufted.

  " Am, Sir, with great refpect,

   " Your very humble Servt,

    " GILBERT LIVINGSTON.

" To Abm. Yates, Jr., Efq.,
 " Prefident of the Con. of N. Y."

On the 21ft of Auguft, Carpenters were much
wanted, and a Letter was addreffed to the Chairman of the Safety Committee at Kingfton to procure them. As the Pay offered was exceedingly
Liberal, we Copy this Letter :

  " POUGHKEEPSIE, Aug. 21ft, 1776.
" SIR :
 " We ftand in need of ten or twelve Carpen-
" ters to execute fome Works for the Defence of
" the Hudfon's River. Take the liberty to requeft

     M

" the Favor of you to procure them immediately
" and Diſpatch them here.   They muſt bring with
" them round Adzes, broad and Wood Axes,
" Gauges, Squares and Compaſſes.   We ſhall al-
" low them 7s 6d and half pint Rum per Day,
" they finding themſelves with other neceſſaries.

" We remain, with reſpeƈt,

" Your humble Servts.,

" CHRISTR. TAPPEN.
" GILBERT LIVINGSTON.

" To John Sleight, Eſq.,
" Chairman of the Com. of Kingſton."

As may be preſumed, this Letter brought the
Carpenters. *Ten* were immediately found by Mr.
Sleight and ſent to Poughkeepſie on the 22d Aug.
The ſecuring of the Carpenters will probably ex-
plain the following order:

" SIR :

" You are hereby ordered to Repair with a
" File of 4 Men under your command, to the
" Storehouſe of Capt. John Schenck, and there
" take out of the ſaid Store two hhds. of Rum
" marked " Congreſs," and take the Guage and
" wantage thereof, and ſend them by the Wagon
" herewith ſent—the one to the Ship Yards and
" the other to the Store-Houſe of Mr. Richd.
" Davis, and this ſhall be your ſufficient Authority

" from the Secret Committee of the State of New
" York.

" CHRIST. TAPPEN.　　⎱ Members
" WILLIAM PAULDING. ⎬ of the
" Poughkeepfie, Aug. 16, 1776. ⎰ Committee.
" To Lieut. Theodorus Brett."

Here is a Bill for Services which fhows the
great Difficulty of fixing the Chain :

" The Secret Committee of the Convention of the
" State of New York,
　　　　　　　　" To Ebenezer Young, Dr.
" 1776.　Expenfes from New York to
" Poughkeepfie, - - - - - - £1　0　0
" Exprefs to Fifhkill, - - - - -　　　6　0
" Board from the 10th Auguft to the
" 25th December, - - - - - 12 13　0
" 141 Days Superintending the fixing
" the Chain and Obftructing the Na-
" vigation at 12s per day, - - - 84 12　0

　　　　　　　　　　£98 11　0

" Errors excepted.　　EBENEZER YOUNG.

" Received, Aug. 10th, 1777, of Mr. Chrifto-
" pher Tappen, one of the Members of the faid
" Committee, ninety-eight Pounds eleven Shillings
" in full of the above Act.
" 98 11.　　　　EBENEZER YOUNG."

A large quantity of the Iron for the Chain was furnifhed by Robt. Livingfton. We have feveral Letters from him to the Committee in regard to the amount fupplied by him. In a Letter dated, " Manor " Livingfton, 11 Auguft, 1776," Mr. Livingfton fays : " I have now brought down to my Wharf " two tuns of Iron, and there is now three tuns " more drawn ready to come down on Tuefday ; " and expect by Saturday to have five tuns more. " All the Iron made fince your laft Orders is 2 inch " and the Bars as long as we could make them." In a Letter dated " Manor Livingfton, Sept. 2, " 1776," Mr. Livingfton renders a Bill of Iron furnifhed to that date. He fays he cannot furnifh the Iron " under £45 per tun, as my Workmen " cannot Work at the fame Wages they have " done ; every Article they want to fupport their " Famileys, being double, and fome Articles, fuch " as Linens, more than double." He farther fays : " You are pleafed to fay that as foon as you have " the whole quantity of Iron you want you will " draw an Order on your Treafurer for the Pay- " ment. I hope that Gentleman does not live " wide of Poughkeepfie, for if he does, I fhould " not chufe in thefe difficult Times to go after " him." The amount of the Bill rendered was £902—or for 22 tons of Iron, about. The total amount of Iron furnifhed by him does not appear. The laft Letter from him bears Date Oct. 6th, 1776, and in this he fpeaks of Iron then being made. Mr. Livingſton's Letters ſhow that Iron was made in different ſized Bars—2, 2½, and 1¼ inch, the former probably for the Chain, and the latter for ſtrengthening the Chain, as appears by the Minutes of Oct. 9th. The Price charged by Mr. Livingſton was regarded by the Convention as exorbitant—£45 per ton—and they gave the matter an Inveſtigation on a Charge that he had ſold Iron to others for £17 and £20; but the Reſult does not appear.

IV.

OBSTRUCTIONS

AT

POLLOPEL'S ISLAND.

THE

OBSTRUCTIONS

AT

POLLOPEL'S ISLAND.

NLIKE thofe at Forts Clinton and Montgomery, the Character of the Obftructions
to the Navigation of the River, extending
from Pollopel's Ifland to a Point near Mur-
derer's Creek, have not been a Matter of un-
certainty. Thofe Obftructions confifted of *Chevaux-de-Frize*[1] formed of fquare Frames of Timber,

[1] CHEVAUX DE FRISE, *(Friefland Horfes*, fo called becaufe firft ufed at the Siege of Groningen, in that Province, in 1658), were at firft armed Beams of fquare Timber or Iron, ufed to defend the Fronts of Camps, Breaches, &c. They were ufually from 15 to 18 feet long, and connected by Chains, each being perforated with fmall Holes, to receive Rods of Wood or Iron, pointed at their Extremities, and, when moved in any Direction, af-fording a fort of Hedge of Spears. (*Enc. Americana*). The *Chevaux de Frife* ufed on this Occafion are

or *Cribs*, from which extended Spars, the Points
of which were armed with Iron, of ſufficient Length
to reach within a few Feet of the Surface of the
Water. The Cribs, or Frames, thus prepared

were loaded with Stone and ſunk at ſuch diſtances
acroſs the Channel as to preſent a Row of Spears
to approaching Veſſels; which Spears, had a Veſſel been run upon them, would have pierced its
Bottom and cauſed it to ſink.

At the Time the Chain at Fort Montgomery
was firſt ſtretched acroſs the River, it broke twice
(as we have ſtated in our previous Article in re-
lation to that Obſtruction). The Failure of this

here frequently called *Caſſoons*, becauſe they were ſupported in Caiſ-
ſons, a kind of Coffer-Dam, conſtructed of Logs and filled with

Stones, as repreſented in the Engraving. The Orthography of theſe
Terms is that of the Original Documents.

Attempt to fix the Chain led to a Conference between Robt. R. Livingſton, Major-Gen. Heath, and Brig. Gen. Clinton (at which Mr. Machin, who in the meantime had been appointed Engineer in the place of Mr. Romans, aſſiſted), in reference to the Obſtrućtions, and to determine what further Steps ſhould be taken. At this Conference, Gen. James Clinton[1] ſuggeſted the ſinking of *Chevaux-*

[1] JAMES CLINTON, the fourth Son of Colonel Charles Clinton, was born Aug. 9th, 1736, at the Reſidence of his Father, in New Windſor, Ulſter County, N. Y. He received an excellent Education, and acquired much Proficiency in the exaćt Sciences; but his ruling Inclination was for a Military Life. He was appointed an Enſign in the Second Regiment of the Militia of Ulſter County, by Sir Charles Hardy, the Governor, and roſe to the Rank of Lieutenant-Colonel in the ſame Regiment, before the commencement of the Revolution. During the War of 1756, between the Engliſh and French, he diſplayed much Courage, and particularly diſtinguiſhed himſelf at the Capture of Fort Frontenac, where he was a Captain under Colonel Bradſtreet, and rendered eſſential Service by taking a Sloop of War on Lake Ontario, which had obſtrućted the Advance of the Army. The Confidence which was repoſed in his Charaćter may be eſtimated by his Appointment as Captain-Commandant of the four Regiments le-

vied for the Protećtion of the Weſtern Frontiers of the Counties of Ulſter and Orange, a Poſt of great Reſponſibility and Danger, as it devolved upon him the protećtion of a Line of Settlements of at leaſt 50 miles in Extent, which were continually threatened by the Savages. (*Encyc. Americana.*) At the Cloſe of the old French War, he retired to his Farm at Little Britain, and married Mary, daughter of Egbert De Witt, a young Lady of great Reſpećtability, whoſe Anceſtors were from Holland. He had four Sons by this Marriage: Alexander, who was Private Secretary to his Uncle, Gov. George Clinton; Charles, who became a Phyſician; De Witt, afterwards the diſtinguiſhed Governor of New York; and George, who was a Lawyer. Gen. Clinton's ſecond Wife was a Mrs. Gray. He had ſeveral Children by this Marriage, one of whom became the Wife of Dr. Francis Bolton, to whoſe Son we are indebted for the Minutes of the Secret Committee; and his Son, James Graham Clinton, repreſented the Orange and Sullivan *de-Frize* at Pollopel's Island. The Conference reported its Proceedings to the Convention, who regarded Gen. Clinton's suggestion with Favour, and appointed Henry Wisner and Gilbert Livingston to take Soundings of the River. On the 22d Nov., 1776, this Committee reported the Result of their Investigations, as follows:

" We have sounded the River, beginning be-

District in Congress for several Years. June 30th, 1775, the War of the Revolution having just commenced, he was appointed, by the Continental Congress, Colonel of the Third Regiment of New York Forces. In the same Year, he marched with Montgomery to Quebec. (*Ibid.*) He was made Brigadier-General, Aug. 9th, 1776. In Oct., 1777, he commanded, under Gov. Clinton, at Fort Clinton, which, with Fort Montgomery, separated from it only by a Creek, defended the Hudson, below West Point, against the Ascent of the Enemy. Sir Henry Clinton, in order to favor the Designs of Burgoyne, attacked these Forts, Oct. 6th, with three thousand Men, and carried them by Storm, they being defended by only about five hundred Militiamen. A brave Resistance was made, from four o'Clock in the Afternoon until dark, when the Garrison was overpowered. (*Allen's Am. Biog. Dict.*) With the utmost Difficulty Gen. Clinton escaped. During the Engagement he received a severe Wound in the Leg, from which he suffered intensely. He reached the Woods, and wandered throughout the Night, enduring extreme Torture. In the Morning he caught a Horse, and rode sixteen Miles before he came to a House, the Inmates of which were startled by the frightful Spectacle he presented, his Regimentals covered with Blood, his Cheeks flushed with Fever, and his Voice hollow and husky. In 1779, with sixteen hundred Men, he joined General Sullivan in his Expedition against the Indians. Proceeding up the Mohawk in Bateaux about fifty-four Miles above Schenectady, he conveyed his Boats by Land, from Canajoharie to the Head of Otsego Lake, one of the Sources of the Susquehanna, down which Stream he must proceed, in order to join Sullivan. As the Water in the Outlet was too low to float his Bateaux, he constructed a Dam across it, and thus accumulated the Water in the Lake. By letting out this Water, and thus suddenly flushing the Stream, his Boats and Troops were rapidly conveyed to Tioga,

" tween Verplanck's and Stoney Point, thence
" Northward through the Highlands to Pollopel's
" Ifland, and find no Part of the River in that
" Diſtance leſs than eighty feet deep in the Main
" Channel, till within a ſhort Diſtance of the If-
" land.
" From the Ifland to the weſtern Shore, found
" by Meaſurement, the Diſtance to be fifty-three

where he found Sullivan, who had
afcended the Sufquehanna. *(Ibid.)*
After one Engagement, in which
the Indians were defeated with great
Loſs, all Reſiſtance on their Part
ceaſed; and, Defolation being
brought home to their own Settlements, they fled to the Britiſh Fortreſs of Niagara; where they died
in great Numbers, in Confequence
of living on falted Proviſions, to
which they were unaccuſtomed.
(Enc. Americana.) It was thought
that this fevere Blow would put a
Stop to further Incurfions by the
Indians. Such, however, unfor-
tunately for the Frontier Settlements, was not the Effect. In the
following Summer their Depredations were renewed, and continued
during the War. *(Marſhall's Waſhington.)* In 1780, Gen. Clinton
was placed in Command of the
Northern Department, with his
Head Quarters at Albany. That
Poſt had been one of great Refpon-
ſibility during the War, and at the
Time of Clinton's appointment had
loſt none of its Importance. The
Spring of 1781, found the Troops

ſtationed there deſtitute of Proviſions, and in a State of Mutiny.
Word was brought to Gen. Clinton
that one of the Companies had refuſed to obey Orders to return to
Quarters. Snatching up his Piſtols
he walked to the Head of the refract-
ory Company, and caſting his Eye
along the Line for a Moment, he
thundered out, " March!" but not
a Soldier ſtirred. Turning to the
Ringleader, he preſented his Piſtol
to his Breaſt, and told him to advance or he would ſhoot him dead
on the Spot. The Captain knew
well what kind of a Man he had to
deal with, and pale with Rage and
Fear, moved on. By Energy and
Refolution the Mutiny was quelled.
In the Winter of 1782, ſome Pro-
motions were made in which junior
Officers took Precedence over Gen.
Clinton. The veteran Soldier could
not brook what he deemed a great
Injury. He folicited and obtained
Leave to withdraw from the active
Duties of the Camp. He made his
laſt Appearance in Arms on the
Evacuation of the City of New
York by the Britiſh, when he bade

" Chains; the Channel near the Middle of the
" River at that Place is about eight Chains broad,
" and fifty feet deep; from the Channel the Water
" fhoals gradually on both fides to the Flats, which
" are about eight or ten Chains broad, reckoning
" both Sides.

" This above defcribed Place is the only one in
" our Opinion, that it is poffible for an Obftruc-
" tion to be made by *docking*, effectually to im-
" pede the Navigation of Hudfon's River, at any
" place above the South Part of the Highlands."

Upon the ftrength of this Report, the Conference determined to adopt General Clinton's Suggeftion.   In a Report to the Committee of Safety,
dated Nov. 26, 1776, they fay :

" It is propofed, with Approbation of the Hon.
" Congrefs, to Obftruct the Navigation in this
" Part by *Caffoons*, which it is conceived will be
" very Practicable."

At the Seffion of the Committee of Safety

an affectionate Farewell to his Com-
mander-in Chief, and retired to his
ample Eftate. He did not, however, enjoy uninterrupted Repofe,
but was often called by his fellow
Citizens to the Performance of civic
Duties. He was one of the Commiffioners to adjuft the boundary
Line between Pennfylvania and New
York; a Member of the Legiflature, and of the Convention which
adopted the prefent Conftitution of
the United States; and a State Senator. All of thefe Offices he filled
with Credit to himfelf, and Ufeful-
nefs to his Country. Gen. Clinton
was of a mild and affectionate Difpofition, but when aroufed by In-
juries and Infults, difplayed extraordinary Energy. In Battle he was
calm and collected. He died Dec.
22, 1812. *(Encyc. Americana.)*

held on that Day, the following Refolution was paffed :

" *Refolved,* That the Navigation of Hudfon's
" River be Obftructed near Pollopel's Ifland at the
" Northern entrance of the Highlands, agreeable
" to the Plan recommended by Gen. James Clin-
" ton,[1] and that the Convention of this State will
" exert every Meafure neceffary for that purpofe."

Up to this Time, the Convention was unwearied in urging upon the Attention of Congrefs and Gen. Wafhington the Importance of giving the Obftructions at Pollopel's Ifland their Attention. Finding that there was little to be hoped for in that Direction, by this Refolution they feem to have determined to go on with the Work at their own Hazard and Expenfe. In accordance with this Determination, at the Seffion of the Convention on the 27th of November a Preamble and Refolution were paffed offering to Gen. Schuyler the Superintendence of the Work. The following is the Refolution :

" *Refolved,* That a Letter be immediately written
" to Major General Schuyler, informing him of
" the Survey that has been taken of Hudfon's River
" at Pollopel's Ifland, and requefting him to take

[1] The Honour of the Suggeftion to employ *Caffoons,* for the Obftruction of the River, clearly belongs to Gen. Schuyler, (fee his Letter in connection with the Fort Mont- gomery Obftructions). Gen. Clin- ton appears to have examined and approved the Plan, and recom- mended its Adoption.

" on himſelf the Superintendence and Direĉtion of
" ſuch Works as he may think Neceſſary, either
" there or elſewhere, for the Security of Hudſon's
" River."

A Letter was accordingly written to Gen. Schuyler, and another to General Waſhington aſking
him to confirm the Appointment of Gen. Schuyler.

At the Seſſion, on the 28th November, Mr.
Duane ſubmitted a Draft of a Letter to Major
General Heath,[1] from which the following is an
Extraĉt :

" We have taken into Conſideration the Plan
" ſuggeſted by Brigadier General Clinton for Ob-
" ſtruĉting the River oppoſite Pollopel's Iſland,

---

[1] WILLIAM HEATH was born
March 2, 1737, at Roxbury, Maſs.,
of which Town one of his Anceſtors
was a Settler in 1636, and was
bred a Farmer. In 1775 he was
appointed Provincial Brigadier, and
alſo Brigadier of the United States,
June 22; and Aug. 9, 1776, Major General. When the Army removed to New York, he commanded near King's Bridge. In
1777 he was intruſted with the
Command of the Eaſtern Department near Boſton, and the Priſon-
ers of Saratoga fell under his Care.
In June, 1779, he returned to the
Main Army, and commanded the
Troops on the Hudſon, and in that
Station, for the moſt Part, he remained until the Cloſe of the War.

In 1793 he was appointed Judge of
Probate for the County of Norfolk.
He was ſeveral Times one of the
Eleĉtors of Preſident. He publiſhed Memoirs of Maj-Gen. Heath,
containing Anecdotes, Details of
Skirmiſhes, Battles, &c., during the
American War, 8vo., 1798. Notwithſtanding the Indications of an
excuſable Vanity and Simplicity, it
exhibits him as an honeſt, faithful
Patriot, and preſents many intereſt-
ing Occurrences of the War. He
ſays of himſelf, " he is of middling
" Stature, light Complexion, very
" corpulent, and bald-headed." He
was the laſt ſurviving Major General
of the War. He died at the place
of his Nativity, Jan. 24, 1814,
aged 77. (Heath's *Memoirs*.)

" and conceiving it to be practicable, we are de-
" termined, with the Permiffion of Congrefs, to
" proceed with the utmoft Vigor to carry it into
" Effect."

At this Stage of the Proceedings, a Conference
was held between Mr. Livingfton, on the Part of
the Convention, and Gens. Heath and Clinton—
the former in Command of the Continental Forces
at Peekfkill, and the latter in Command of the
Forces in the Highlands—in reference to the Obftructions. The Refult of this Conference was
reported to the Convention by Mr. Livingfton, at
its Seffion on the 30th November, as appears by
the Minutes, as follows:

" Mr. Livingfton informed the Convention that
" he had Conferred with Major General Heath
" and Brigadier General Clinton about Obftructing
" Hudfon's River at Pollopel's Ifland (at which
" Conference Mr. Machin affifted), that it appeared
" to them to be extremely Practicable, and that he
" had the pleafure of affuring the Convention that
" both Generals feemed ftrongly impreffed with a
" Senfe of the Importance of that Work and de-
" termined to give every Affiftance in their Power
" to perfect the fame, or rather to *take it upon*
" *themfelves*, which His Excellency Gen. Wafh-
" ington's orders on that Head (which Gen. Heath
" was fo obliging as to Communicate to Mr.
" Livingfton), happily enabled them to do.

O

"That in this Conference it was determined
"that 500 Men, under the Command of Brig.
"Gen. Clinton, ſhould this Day March for Fort
"Conſtitution, in order to begin the Work on Sun-
"day Morning, in caſe they can be provided with
"300 Axes by this Convention, all other Tools
"having been furniſhed by the Continental Stores."

Upon Mr. Livingſton's Suggeſtion, a Series of
Reſolutions were adopted extending to Generals
Heath and Clinton every Aſſiſtance in the Power
of the Convention. Mr. Cuyler and Mr. Duer
were authorized and directed "to Employ ſuch
"and ſo many Perſons as they ſhall think fit, to
"Purchaſe and Collect 300 felling Axes; and that
"they have Power to impreſs the ſame where
"there is more than one in a Family," that the
Perſons ſo employed "ſet out on this Buſineſs im-
"mediately and return all the Axes they ſhall
"obtain this Day to Gen. Clinton at New Wind-
"ſor, by 7 o'Clock on Sunday Morning." Boats
were alſo ordered collected for carrying Stone and
that "the Boats be delivered to Gen. Clinton, or
"his Agent (Mr. Machin), at New Windſor."
The Timber which had been collected at Poughkeepſie for the Fort Montgomery Obſtruction was
ordered to be "immediately rafted to New Wind-
"ſor."[1] Gilbert Livingſton was directed to cauſe

---

[1] Among the Clinton Papers we
find the following Letter to Mr.
Livingſton, one of the Secret Committee, in reference to the Timber
and Iron here referred to:

" three tons of Iron of an inch and a half, and one
" inch and three quarters thick, or fuch other
" quantities and fizes as Gen. Clinton may direct,
" to be delivered as foon as poffible at New Wind-
" for," and £400 were appropriated to " defray

" NEW WINDSOR,
" 12th Dec , 1776.

"DEAR SIR—Laft Night Mr. Ebenezer Young arrived here with a Raft of Timber faid to contain 74 Logs of thirty Feet long and upwards, and 67 of about 13 or 14 Feet, and a Quantity of Ropes, Anchors, &c. For the Latter he will deliver you the Engineer's Receipt. As to the Timber a great Part of it is fo Short that it cannot be of any Ufe to us in making Blocks to obftruct the Navigation of the River, having, before it arrived, got a Sufficiency of that Length. Had it been fent fooner, we might have ufed it to Advantage. The longer Logs may be ufed in this Bufinefs, but I am informed that moft if not all of them have been procured at fuch an extravagant Price that I can't, without particular Directions from the Honorable the Convention, think of doing it. Timber we can get at little Expenfe indeed, by the Soldiery, fafter than we can poffibly work is up on Blocks—at the higheft Computation not to exceed 5s a Log for thofe quite as Good for our Purpofe as any in the Raft. This being the Cafe, I fhould not be able to Juftify the ufing them in the Raft at the immoderate Price of five or fix

Pounds a Piece, which I have been informed they coft you. I have, however, ordered the Raft to be laid upon Ellifon's Cove, and fecured there that it may be employed here or fent back to Poughkeepfie, as your Committee or the Convention fhall direct. Perhaps it may be applied to fome other Purpofe that will better juftify the Ufe of fuch high priced Timber. The Iron you fent—except the quantity I applied for and of the Size—I don't imagine we fhall be able to ufe. If, therefore, you think you can difpofe of it at Poughkeepfie, I will order it back—which I fhould have done immediately had not the Veffel that brought it been taken to carry part of the Northern Troops to Haverftraw. It is Safe in Store, and if I poffibly can Ufe it or difpofe of it to any Advantage for you I will.

"I am your moft obdt. Servt.,
" GEO. CLINTON.
" To Gilbert Livingfton, Efq."

In the Fort Montgomery Article the Reader will have noticed the Bill of White & Livingfton, for Logs, of which thefe were probably a Part. We infer that thefe Logs were fubfequently ufed in the Weft Point Chain.

"the expenses thereof." This Action rendered unneceffary the appointment of Gen. Schuyler— Gens. Heath and Clinton having taken the Work upon themfelves—and hence a Copy of the Refo- lutions paffed were forwarded to him, together with a Refolution that " Major General Schuyler " be requefted to meet and confult with Gen. " Clinton on the Plan for Obftructing Hudfon's " River near Pollopel's Ifland."

From thefe Proceedings it will be feen that the Obftructions at Pollopel's Ifland were under the immediate Superintendence of Gen. Geo. Clinton. The place felected for the Conftruction of the *Chevaux-de-Frize* was at New Windfor, where re- mains of the Forges ftill exift. The Troops re- ferred to by Mr. Livingfton, in his Statement to the Convention, arrived at Fort Conftitution at the Time appointed, and the felling of Timber for the Conftruction of the *Chevaux-de-Frize* imme- diately commenced.[1] From this Time we find

[1] The following Letter from Gen. Clinton to the Convention, fhows the Commencement of the Work:

" FORT CONSTITUTION,
" 1ft Dec. 1776.

" SIR—I arrived here Yefterday Evening with two Regiments, con- fifting of about 500 Men, deftined for garrifoning this Fort, and Ob- ftructing the Navigation of the River near Polopin's Ifland, agree- able to the Refolve of the Conven- tion. I immediately fent off the Engineer with about one hundred Men to get Timber for the pur- pofe, but I am fo unfortunate as not to have Axes for the tenth Part of the number, though I have ufed my beft Endeavors to procure as many as I poffibly could. Axes, there- fore, three or four light Anchors and Cables, Drag Ropes, Screws, Scows and other Boats for collect- ing of Stones I muft beg the Con- vention will endeavor to Supply me with as quick as poffible. The Bufinefs otherwife muft in a great Meafure ftand ftill. I have Smiths

the Convention acting in conjunction with Gens. Heath and Clinton in conftructing the Work. On the 4th of December, Gen. Clinton forwarded to the Convention the following Memoranda of Articles wanted:

"Wanted by the Detachment employed in Ob-
"ftructing the Navigation of Hudfon's River, near

employed in making Axes, and I fhall make them Work Day and Night to replace thofe you may Supply me with; and when Gen. Lee's Divifion paffes the River, and they are now at Peekfkill, we fhall be able to get a number of Boats from that Quarter, but for the prefent we muft be Supplied by Convention if poffible. I have about 40 Artificers, which are as many as can well be employed, and being furnifhed with the above Articles only, I hope I fhall be able to carry on the Work without troubling your Honorable Houfe in fome Time for any other Supplies.

"Capt. Bedlow has hitherto acted here as a Commiffary of Stores, and Mr. Lawrence as Clerk of the Check, and as there are no other Perfons appointed to take charge of the Stores, Tools, &c., or keep the Accounts which will be neceffarily multiplied by this bufinefs, I am of opinion it will be beft to continue them. I am fure if they do their Duty, as I don't doubt they will, they will fave ten Times more than their Wages; efpecially as it will be out

of my Power to do my own Duty and attend particularly to that Part of the Bufinefs.

"The Bearer, Capt. Bedlow, who will wait your Anfwer and bring down fuch of the wanted Articles as you can furnifh us with, will inform you of the Scandalous Manner fome of the Militia left this Place, without returning the Ammunition or other Public Stores they had been furnifhed with.

"Mr. Livingfton gave me Reafon to hope I fhould have three Companies of Rangers join me; I wifh to have them, as we fhall want all the Aid the Convention can give us, and I have a ftrong defire to Work thofe Gentry a little. If they fhould object againft going out of their County, as I have heard they do, I'll fix them in it. They will be equally convenient to the Work.

"I am with due refpect,
"Your moft obt. Servt.,
"Geo. Clinton.
"To the Honorable the Prefident of the Convention, of the State of New York."

" Pollopen's Iſland, ſix thouſand Bricks for Forges
" for Blackſmith's Shops; and a few Ovens to
" bake Bread in for the Soldiers. The Logs at
" Poughkeepſie ought to be brought down," &c.

At a Meeting of the Convention held Jan. 6th,
1777, the following Reſolution was paſſed :

" *Reſolved,* That Capt. Machin be empowered,
" with the Advice and under the Direction of Gen.
" George Clinton,[1] to employ ſuch and ſo many

[1] GEORGE CLINTON was the youngeſt Son of Col. Charles Clinton, and was born in Ulſter County, now Orange, July 26, 1739. He was named after the Colonial Governor, a Friend of his Father. In his Education his Father was aſſiſted by Daniel Thain, a Miniſter from Scotland. In early Life he evinced the enterpriſe which diſtinguiſhed him afterwards. He once left his Father's Houſe and ſailed in a Privateer. On his Return he accompanied as a Lieutenant his Brother, James, in the Expedition againſt Fort Frontenac, now Kingſton. He afterwards ſtudied Law under William Smith, and roſe to ſome Diſtinction in his native County. As a Member of the Colonial Aſſembly in 1775 and afterwards, he was a zealous Whig. May 15, 1775, he took his Seat as a Member of Congreſs. He voted for the Declaration of Independence, July 4, 1776; but, being called away by his appointment as Brigadier General before the Inſtrument was ready for the Signature of the Members, his Name is not attached to it. March 25, 1777, he was appointed Brigadier General of the United States. At the firſt Election under the Conſtitution of New York, he was choſen, April 20, 1777, both Governor and Lieutenant Governor. Accepting the former office, the latter was filled by Mr. Van Cortlandt. He was thus elected Chief Magiſtrate ſix ſucceſſive Periods, or for eighteen Years, till 1795, when he was ſucceeded by Mr. Jay. Being at the Head of a Powerful State, and in the command of the Militia, his Patriotic Services were of the higheſt importance to his Country. On the advance of the Enemy up the Hudſon in Oct., 1777, he Prorogued the Aſſembly and proceeded to take command of Fort Montgomery, where he and his Brother James made a moſt gallant Defence Oct. 6th. He eſcaped under cover

" Laborers and Artificers as will be fufficient to per-
" feƈt the Obſtruƈtions in Hudſon's River, and to
" lay out and ereƈt ſuch Works as will be neceſſary
" for the Defence thereof."

The Works here referred to were evidently
thoſe at Plumb Point, remains of which, in a re-
markable ſtate of Preſervation, ſtill exiſt on the
Property of P. A. Verplanck, Eſq., New Windſor.

of the Night. The next Day Forts Independence and Conſtitution were evacuated, He preſided in the Convention at Poughkeepſie, June 17, 1788, for deliberating on the Federal Conſtitution, which he deemed not ſufficiently guarded in favor of the Sovereignty of each State. After being five Years in Private Life, he was elected to the Legiſlature. Again in 1801 was he choſen Governor, but in 1804 was ſucceeded by Mr. Lewis. In that Year he was elevated to the Vice Preſidency of the United States, in which Station he continued till his Death. It was by his caſting Vote that the Bill for renewing the Bank Charter was negatived. In Private Life he was frank, amiable, and warm in Friendſhip. By his Wife, Cornelia Tappan, of King-ſton, he had one Son and five Daughters. He died at Waſhington April 20, 1812, aged 72. An Oration on his Death was delivered by Governeur Morris.

Of his Energy and Deciſion the following are Inſtances. At the Concluſion of the War, when a Britiſh Officer was placed on a Cart in the City of New York, to be tarred and feathered, he ruſhed in among the Mob with a drawn Sword and reſcued the Sufferer. During the raging of what was called the Doctor's Mob, when, in Conſequence of the Diſinterment of ſome Bodies for Diſſeƈtion, the Houſes of the Phyſicians were in Danger of being pulled down, he called out the Militia and quelled the Turbulence. The following is an Inſtance of the Skill with which he diverted Attention from his grow-ing Infirmities. On a viſit to Pittsfield, as he was riſing from a Dinner Table in his old Age, he fell, but was caught by a Lady ſitting next to him. " Thus," ſaid he, " ſhould I ever wiſh to fall—into the Hands of the Ladies." For many Years he ſuffered much by the Rhumatiſm. (*Delaplaine's Repoſitory; Encyclopedia America-na ; Almon's Remembrancer,* 1780, 160; See Street's *Council of Revi-ſion*).

We have no further recorded Action in reference to the Obftructions until the 12th of March, 1777, when a Committee, appointed for that purpofe, reported to the Convention that they had

"Waited upon Gen. Geo. Clinton, and were "informed by him that the Obftruction of the "Navigation is in great forwardnefs; a number of "Frames and Blocks are ready for finking," &c., and that "thofe Works will be completed by the "Middle of April."

At the Meeting of the Convention held April 26, 1777, two thoufand Pounds were appropriated "for the ufe of the Works carrying on to Obftruct "the Navigation in Hudfon's River near Pollopel's "Ifland."

We find nothing fhowing the precife Time at which the *Chevaux-de-Frize* were placed in the River. That a Portion of them were there when the Expedition under Vaughan[1] and Wallace paffed

---

[1] JOHN VAUGHAN, K. B., was Son of the Second Lord Lifburne, of the Peerage of Ireland. He entered the Army in 1748, and became Captain in the 17th Regiment of Foot in 1756; Lieutenant Colonel unattached in January, 1760, and was appointed to the 46th or South Devonfhire Regiment of Foot, ferving in America, in November, 1762, of which Regiment he was commiffioned Colonel, on 11th May, 1775. He was ap- pointed Major General in America 1ft January, 1776, and was fecond in command of the Britifh Referve at the Battle on Staten Ifland, on the 1ft Auguft of that Year. Maj. Gen. Vaughan commanded about 1200 Men who were directed to march towards Fort Clinton on the 6th Oct., and cover Corps under Lt. Col. Campbell. By the Britifh Account, the Approaches to the Fort were through a continued Abbatis of near 400 Yards in

up the River is evident from the following in the Letter from Gov. Clinton to the Convention announcing the Reduction of the Forts: "As foon "as I find the Shipping are likely to pafs the *Che-* "*vaux-de-Frize*, I will, by a forced March, endea- "vour to gain Kingfton and cover that Town."

In a Letter dated Little Britain, Oct 12, 1777, Gov. Clinton fays that the Enemy are deftroying the Works at Forts Clinton and Montgomery;

Length, defenfive in its whole Courfe, and expofed to the Fire of 10 Pieces of Cannon. (*Beatfon,* IV, 236). On the 14th Oct. Maj. Gen. Vaughan, with a Body of Troops in Bateaux, efcorted by Sir James Wallace's Squadron, proceeded up the River to Kingfton, where they had been informed there were confiderable Stores, On the 15th, finding that Trenches had been thrown up and every Difpofition made to annoy them, Gen. Vaughan determined to attack them before they fhould have Time to ftrengthen their Works, or to collect Reinforcements. He therefore landed his Detachment, affailed the Batteries, and having driven the Americans from their Works, and fpiked or deftroyed their Guns, he advanced directly to the Town, at the Entrance of which he found a Body of Men, with Small Arms and Artillery, drawn up to oppofe him. Thefe he routed and feized their Cannon. On entering the Town his Men were fired upon from the Houfes, whereupon he gave Orders to fet the Town on Fire, and it was entirely confumed, together with a confiderable Quantity of Military Stores. The American Shipping was alfo all deftroyed, except an armed Galley, which ran up the Creek. Finding that a Junction with Gen. Burgoyne's Army was impracticable, the combined Armament returned to New York. (*Ib.*, 237-38). His Regiment formed part of the Expedition under General Grant to the Weft Indies in 1777, and he was appointed Commander-in-Chief of the Forces in the Leeward Iflands. In 1779, when the Britifh paffed the *Chevaux-de-Frize*, he invefted Fort Lafayette, which furrendered on the 2d June in that Year. (*Ib.* 503-4). In 1781, he accompanied the Expedition againft the Dutch Weft India Poffeffions. He was next appointed Governor of Berwick, and Lieutenant General in 1782. He died Colonel of the 46th Regiment, 30th June, 1795. (*N. Y. Col. Hift.*, VII, 749).

P

and, in a Poftfcript to this Letter, he fays : " Yef-
" terday Evening an armed Schooner, two Row
" Galleys and a fmall Brig paffed the *Chevaux-de-*
" *Frize*, and are out of Sight up the River this
" Morning."

But the Works were not entirely completed
until the fubfequent Year, as we find Gov. Clinton
writing under date of Jan. 17th, 1778 : " I would
" advife, that the *Chevaux-de-Frize* be completed
" under the Directions of Capt. Machin, who has
" hitherto had the Management of that Bufinefs.
" He knows how many are yet wanted, and where
" to be funk, fo as to perfect the Obftructions."

V.

OBSTRUCTIONS

AT

WEST POINT.

THE

OBSTRUCTIONS

AT

WEST POINT.

HE Obftructions to the Navigation of Hudfon's River at Weft Point, were placed there in the Spring of 1778. Immediately after the return of Sir Henry Clinton's[1] Expedition to New York, the more thorough Fortification of the Highlands was urged by Gen. Wafhington, who in a Letter dated December 2d,

[1] HENRY CLINTON, K. B., was the eldeft Son of Admiral George Clinton, formerly Governor of the Province of New York (*New York Colonial Hift.*, vi, 475), and Grandfon of the 6th Earl of Lincoln. He entered the Army early in Life, having been appointed during his Father's Adminiftration, Captain Lieutenant of the New York Companies. He became Lieutenant in the Coldftream Guards 1ft Nov., 1751; and was promoted to Captain of a Company in the 1ft Foot Guards 6th May, 1758. (*Mackennon's Coldftream Guards*, 11, 487).

1777, inſtructed Gen. Putnam to conſult with Gov. Clinton, Gen. Parſons, and the French Engineer, Colonel Radière, with a view to the Erection of ſuch " Works and Obſtructions as may be " neceſſary to defend and ſecure the River againſt " any future attempts of the Enemy."[1] The following is Waſhington's Letter :

In 1762 he became Colonel in the Army, and of the 12th Regiment of Foot on the 28th November, 1766. After gaining great Credit by his Services during the Seven Years' War in Germany, he roſe to the Rank of Major General 25th May, 1772, and in May, 1775, arrived at Boſton. In June he diſtinguiſhed himſelf at Bunker Hill, and was rewarded, on the 1ſt of September following, by being created Knight of the Bath and advanced to the Rank of Lieutenant General in America. On 1ſt January, 1776, he was appointed General in America, and was defeated that Year at Sullivan's Iſland; commanded the Firſt Line of the Britiſh Army at Staten Iſland 1ſt Auguſt; on the 27th of the ſame Month, commanded a Diviſion in the Battle on Long Iſland; in October, defeated a Portion of the American Army on the Bronx, in Weſtcheſter County; and in December, and againſt his will, was ſent to take Poſſeſſion of Rhode Iſland. In 1777, he was engaged in Operations on the Hudſon River for the Relief of Burgoyne; was appointed Lieutenant General in the Army in Auguſt, and in October was preſent at the Storming of Forts Montgomery and Clinton. In 1778, Sir Henry Clinton was commiſſioned Commander-in-Chief, and conducted the Retreat from Philadelphia to New York; was appointed Colonel of the 84th Royal Highlanders in December, of the ſame Year. In April, 1779, became Colonel of the 7th Light Dragoons, and in December embarked for Charleſton, which he reduced. He was ſucceeded in the Chief Command by General Carleton in 1782, when he returned to England, where he publiſhed a *Narrative of his Conduct in America*, 1782; *Obſervations on the Earl Cornwallis's Anſwer*, 1783; *Letter to the Commiſſioner of Public Accounts*, 1784; and *Obſervations on Mr. Stedman's Hiſtory of the American War*, 1794. He died 13th December, 1795. (*N. Y. Col. Hiſt.*, VIII, 717).

[1] Sparks, v, 177.

" Head Quarters, 2 December, 1777.
" Dear Sir :
" The importance of the Hudſon River in
" the preſent Conteſt, and the neceſſity of defend-
" ing it, are Subjeɛts which have been ſo frequently
" and fully difcuſſed, and are ſo well underſtood,
" that it is unneceſſary to enlarge upon them.
" Theſe Faɛts at once appear, when it is conſidered
" that it runs through a whole State; that it is
" the only Paſſage by which the Enemy from
" New York, or any Part of our Coaſt, can ever
" hope to coöperate with an Army from Canada;
" that the poſſeſſion of it is indiſpenſably eſſential
" to preſerve the Communication between the
" Eaſtern, Middle and Southern States; and fur-
" ther, that upon its Security, in a great Meaſure, ·
" depend our chief Supplies of Flour for the ſub-
" ſiſtence of ſuch Forces, as we may have occaſion
" for, in the courſe of the War, either in the Eaſt-
" ern or Northern Departments, or in the Country
" lying high up on the Weſt ſide of it. Theſe
" Faɛts are familiar to all; they are familiar to you.
" I therefore requeſt you, in the moſt urgent
" Terms, to turn your moſt ſerious and aɛtive At-
" tention to this infinitely important objeɛt. Seize
" the preſent opportunity, and employ your whole
" Force and all the Means in your Power· for
" ereɛting and completing, as far as it ſhall be
" poſſible, ſuch Works and Obſtruɛtions as may be
" neceſſary to defend and ſecure the River againſt

" any future attempts of the Enemy. You will
" confult Governor Clinton, General Parfons,[1] and

[1] SAMUEL HOLDEN PARSONS, was
born at Lyme, Conn., 14th May,
1737, and was graduated at Harvard in 1756; was admitted to the
Bar in 1759, and fettled at Lyme
in the Practice of the Law; married
in 1761; was Member of the General Affembly from 1762 to 1774,
during which Time he filled various
Appointments of Honour and Truft,
among which was that of fettling
the Boundary of the Connecticut
Claim on the Border of Pennfylvania. In 1773 he was appointed
one of the Standing Committee of
Correfpondence and Inquiry with
the Sifter Colonies, of which he was
an energetick Member, and origin-
ated the Suggeftion of affembling
the Firft Congrefs which fubfequently met at New York; an Act
which led to the Continental Congrefs, to the Confederation, and that
great Chain of Events, connected
with the War of Independence. In
Nov. 1773, he was appointed King's
Attorney. In 1775, he with a few
Connecticut Gentlemen formed the
bold Defign, which was fuccefsfully
executed, of feizing Ticonderoga
and Crown Point, the firft *offenfive*
Blow ftruck by the Colonies. He
had been appointed Major of the
Fourteenth Regiment of Militia in
1770, and on the 26th April, 1775,
was commiffioned Colonel of the
Sixth Regiment, raifed for the fpecial
Defence and Safety of the Colony,
and foon after marched to and con-

tinued at Roxbury, until the Britifh
evacuated Bofton, when he was
ordered to New York. He was
actively engaged at the Battle of
Long Ifland, Aug. 1776. (See
Botta; Williams's *Life Olney;* Stiles's
Diary.) In Aug. 1776, he was
appointed by Congrefs Brigadier
General, and was with the Army
at Harlem Heights, Kingfbridge,
and in the Battle of White Plains.
He was fubfequently ftationed at
Peekfkill with a Portion of the Army
to protect the important Pofts upon
the North River, and from thence
was frequently detached upon various Expeditions. In May, 1777,
he planned the eminently fuccefsful
and important Expedition of Col.
Meigs to Sagg Harbour (Marfhall's
Life Wafh., III, 96), in June following reinforced Wafhington in
New Jerfey; and on the Retreat of
Gen. Howe was detached to Peekfkill, when, at his urgent Solicitation,
the Highlands were ftrongly reinforced, but before effectual Meafures
were confummated, Gen. Clinton
with a ftrong Force captured all
the Defences and paffed above the
Highlands. In the Winter of 1777,
fuffering under feeble Health, and
a Conftitution broken down in the
Service, Gen. Parfons expreffed to
the Commander-in-Chief a Defire
to retire temporarily from the active
Duties of the Army; but at the
urgent Solicitation of Wafhington,
he determined to continue at the

" the French Engineer, Colonel Radière, upon
" the occaſion. By gaining the Paſſage, you know

Head of his Brigade. In the beginning of 1778 he took Command of
the Troops ſtationed at the Highlands, with the additional Duty of
conſtructing Military Works at Weſt
Point. In a Letter to Waſhington,
dated 16th March, 1778, he ſays:
" I ſhall pay particular Attention
" to forwarding the Work of the
" Boats deſigned for tranſporting
" over, as well as to thoſe which
" are to be employed for Defenſe
" on Hudſon River. I have or-
" dered all the Boats and other
" Crafts on the River to be collected
" in different Places, and put in the
" beſt poſſible State immediately.
" When I was laſt at Poughkeepſie
" the Gun-Boats were in ſuch a
" State as to give Hopes of their
" being fit for Uſe within a few
" Weeks ; and as Gov. Clinton has
" been kind enough to take upon
" himſelf the Direction of them, I
" think we may hope to ſee them
" completed ſoon. I will ſend to
" Albany, and know the State of
" the Boats there, and as the River
" will be ſoon Clear of Ice, I will
" order down ſuch Boats and other
" Crafts as can be had there, fit for
" Tranſportation over the River.
" If the Chain is complete, we ſhall
" be ready to ſtretch it over the
" River next Week. A ſufficient
" Number of the *Chevaux-de-Frize*
" to fill thoſe Parts left Open laſt
" Year, are ready to ſink as ſoon
" as the Weather and the State of

" the River will admit it to be done.
" I hope to have two Sides and one
" Baſtion of the Fort in ſome State
" of Defence in about a Fortnight.
" The other Sides need very little to
" ſecure them. There is a Proſpect
" of having five or ſix Cannon
" mounted in one of our Batteries
" this Week. I think the Works
" are going on as faſt as could be
" expected from our ſmall Number
" of Men, total Want of Materials
" provided, and of Money to pur-
" chaſe them. We have borrowed
" and begged and hired Money to this
" Time. I have ſeveral Times ad-
" vanced my laſt Shilling towards
" purchaſing Materials, &c.; and I
" believe this has been the Caſe with
" almoſt every Officer here. As we
" ſtill live, I hope we ſhall accompliſh
" the Works in the River in Seaſon,
" if the Enemy move with their
" accuſtomed Caution and Tardi-
" neſs; when I hope Congreſs will
" repay what has been advanced,
" and cannot think us blamable if
" we have been compelled to ſave
" the Public Credit, and forward the
" Buſineſs intruſted to our Care."

From the above Correſpondence
it appears that the Fortifications at
Weſt Point, and upon the Highlands,
were for a Time under the Superintendence of Gen. Parſons, where
he was ſtationed the principal Part
of the Years 1778 and 1779, but
was frequently Detached upon Expeditions to protect the Sea-coaſt

Q

" the Enemy have already laid waſte and deſtroyed
" all the Houſes, Mills and Towns acceſſible to

of his native State, near Horſeneck, Greenwich, New Haven and New London. Time and Space, how-ever, will not permit a full Statement of his Services. It appears, alſo, from his numerous Opinions, re-corded and preſerved among the Manuſcripts of Gen. Waſhington, that he was frequently conſulted in Queſtions of great Moment, and in critical Times of Publick Danger. In 1779, he was ſtationed oppoſite Weſt Point with Inſtructions to aſſiſt in conſtructing the Works. In July of that Year, Gen. Tryon having invaded Connecticut with 2600 Men, Gen. Parſons, at the Head of 150 Continental Troops and the Militia under Gen. Wol-cott, attacked the Britiſh on the Morning of the 12th July, ſoon after they landed at Norwalk, and although too Weak to prevent the Deſtruction of that Fort, he har-raſſed the Enemy ſo much during the Day, that they retired for freſh Reinforcements, and finally aban-doned the Undertaking of penetrat-ing that State. On the 29th Oct, 1780, he was one of the Board which tried Major Andre; and in the ſame Month received from Con-greſs a Commiſſion as Major Gene-ral, and ſucceeded Gen. Putnam in the Command of the Connecticut Line of the Continental Army. The defenceleſs Inhabitants between Greenwich and New York, having been much annoyed, and ſuffered

great Loſſes by the frequent Incur-ſions of Col. Delancy's Corps at Morriſiaña, Gen. Parſons deter-mined to deſtroy the Enemy's Bar-racks, which could not be rebuilt during the Winter; and thus afford ſome Protection to the Inhabitants in that Vicinity. For this Purpoſe, he advanced, with rapid Marches, to Weſt Cheſter and Morriſiana, with a few Continentals, attacked the Britiſh Troops, and effectually accompliſhed his Object.. Congreſs now paſſed a Reſolution directing Gen Waſhington to preſent to Gen. Parſons and the Officers under his Command, the Thanks of Congreſs for his judicious Arrangements, and for the Courage diſplayed by the Officers and Men. In the Year 1781, he was appointed by the Governor and Council of Connect-icut to command the State Troops and Coaſt Guards, raiſed for the Protection of the State, and to diſ-poſe them in ſuch Manner as he ſhould judge expedient to protect the Inhabitants from the Incurſions of the Enemy on the Sea-coaſt. At the Cloſe of the War he reſumed the Practice of the Law in Middle-town, whither his Family had been removed during the Revolution, and frequently repreſented that Town in the Legiſlature. In the Proſecu-tion of Meaſures for the Formation of Middleſex County, he was more engaged and more influential than any other Man. He was an active

" them. Unleſs proper Meaſures are taken to pre-
" vent them, they will renew their Ravages in the
" Spring, or as ſoon as the Seaſon will admit, and

and influential Member of the State Convention which aſſembled at Hartford, January, 1781, and adopted the Conſtitution of the United States. He was a Member and for ſome Time Preſident of the Society of Cincinnati, in Connecticut. In the latter Part of the Year 1785, he was appointed by Congreſs, a Commiſſioner, in Connection with Gens. Richard Butler of Pittsburg, and George Rogers Clarke of Kentucky, to treat with the Shawanoe Indians, near the Falls of Ohio, for extinguiſhing the Aboriginal Title to certain Lands within the Northweſtern Territory. This Treaty was held on the northweſtern Bank of the Ohio, near the Mouth of the Great Miama, January 31ſt, 1786, and the Indians then ceded to the United States a large and valuable Tract upon which the flouriſhing City of Cincinnati now ſtands. Under the Ordinance of Congreſs of 1787, he was appointed Judge in and over the Territory of the United States northweſt of the River Ohio. The Commiſſion is dated October 23d, 1787, and ſigned by Arthur St. Clair, Preſident, and Charles Thomſon, Secretary of Congreſs. In 1789, he was nominated by Gen. Waſhington, by and with the Conſent of the Senate, Chief Judge in and over the ſame Territory, then embracing the preſent States of Ohio, Indiana, Illinois and Michigan, which Office he held until his Death. In 1789, he was appointed by the State of Connecticut a Commiſſioner, with Gov. Wolcott, and Hon. James Davenport, to hold a Treaty with the Wyandots and other Tribes of Indians for extinguiſhing their Claim to the Lands called the Connecticut Weſtern Reſerve, and in the Fall of 1789 he viſited that Country with a View to preliminary Arrangements for holding a Treaty with them. While returning to his Reſidence at Marietta, he was drowned in deſcending the Rapids of the Big Beaver River, the 17th of November, 1789, aged fifty-two years. Among the Manuſcripts of Gen. Parſons in the Poſſeſſion of his Grandſon, Samuel H. Parſons, of Middletown, are a Journal of Obſervations and Occurrences when he firſt viſited the Weſtern Country; a Communication to the American Academy of Arts and Sciences in October, 1786, deſcribing the Weſtern Mounds, Manners and Cuſtoms of the Aborigines; Original Addreſs to the Shawanoe Tribes; beſides a voluminous Correſpondence before, during, and after the Revolutionary War, with the diſtinguiſhed Men of that Period. *(Hildreth's Lives of the Early Settlers of Ohio; N. E. Hiſt. Gen. Regiſter, etc.)*

" perhaps Albany, the only Town in the State of
" any importance remaining in our Hands, may
" undergo a like Fate, and a general Havoc and
" Devaftation take place.

" To prevent thefe Evils, therefore, I fhall ex-
" pect that you will exert every Nerve, and employ
" your whole Force in Future, while and when-
" ever it is practicable, in conftructing and for-
" warding the proper Works and Means of Defence.
" The Troops muft not be kept out on Command,
" and acting in Detachments to cover the Country
" below, which is a Confideration infinitely lefs
" important and interefting.

" I am, Dear Sir, &c."

In a Letter to Gov. Clinton of the fame Date,
Gen. Wafhington expreffed much Solicitude on
the Subject.   Gov. Clinton, in Reply, affured the
Commander-in-Chief of his hearty Concurrence
in any Effort that might be agreed upon; and he
gave feveral important Hints refpecting the Conftruction of new Works on the River, and efpecially recommended, that a " ftrong Fortrefs fhould
" be erected at Weft Point oppofite to Fort Con-
" ftitution."[1]

On the fame date, Wafhington alfo addreffed a
Letter to Major General Gates, directing him,

---

[1] This was probably the firft
Suggeftion, from any official Source,
which led to the Fortification of
that important Pofition, although
the Plan of Fortifications at that
Place had been difcuffed at the
Time of agreeing to the Conftruction of Forts Montgomery and
Clinton.

" with a certain Part of the Northern Army and
" the Aſſiſtance of the Militia of New York and
" the Eaſtern States, to attempt the Recovery of the
" Poſts upon the North River from the Enemy,
" and to put them if recovered in the beſt
" Poſture of Defence." But Gen. Gates was appointed, at about the ſame Time, Preſident of the
Board of War, and did not act in the Matter.
Waſhington alſo addreſſed a Letter to Gov. Clinton requeſting him " to take the Chief Direction
" and Superintendence of this Buſineſs." Gov.
Clinton replied that he would coöperate with any
one charged with the Chief Direction of the
Works, but in Conſideration of his other Duties
muſt decline the Appointment.

The Matter thus remained under the Direction
of Gen. Putnam, who, early in January, 1778,
brought the Subject before the Provincial Convention of New York, as appears from the following Proceedings:

" THURSDAY, Jan. 8, 1778.

" Application being made by Major General
" Putnam, Commanding Officer of the Middle
" Department, that this Convention would appoint
" a Committee to confer with him relative to the
" neceſſary Works to be conſtructed for the De-
" fences of the Paſſes in the Highlands.

" *Reſolved,* That the General's requeſt be com-
" plied with, and that Mr. Scott, Mr. Pawling,
" Mr. Wiſner, Mr. Snyder, Mr. Killian Van

" Renffelaer, Mr. Drake, Mr. Hathorn, and Mr.
" Hoffman, be a Committee for that Purpofe."[1]

" FRIDAY, Jan. 9, 1778.

" General Scott, from the Committee appointed
" Yefterday Evening, to confer with Gen. Putnam
" and Gen. James Clinton, the Lieutenant Colonel
" of Engineers and other Military Officers, relative
" to the neceffary Works to be conftructed for the
" Paffes in the Highlands, and the Place or Places
" where the fame ought to be erected, reported
" that they had conferred with the faid Generals
" and other Officers; that on fuch Conference
" there was a difagreement in Sentiment between
" thofe Gentlemen (arifing from certain different
" Facts alleged), as to the place where fuch Works
" ought to be erected; and, therefore, that it was
" the Opinion of the faid Committee and the Mi-
" litary Gentlemen, that this Convention appoint
" Commiffioners to view the feveral Paffes on
" Hudfon River, with the Generals and other
" Officers, and advife in fixing the places where
" fuch Fortifications fhould be erected.

" *Refolved*, That John Slofs Hobart, Efq.,[2] one

---

[1] Jour. Prov. Con., 1113.

[2] JOHN SLOSS HOBART was born
in Fairfield, Conn., February,
1738, and was graduated at Yale
College, 1757; joined the Sons of
Liberty in New York in Nov.,
1765, which were organifed to oppofe the Execution of the Stamp
Act; in 1775 was Member of the
Provincial Convention from Suffolk
County, and was Deputy from the
fame County to the Provincial
Congrefs held in 1775 and 1776,
alfo to the Convention of Reprefentatives in 1777, which formed

"of the Justices of the Supreme Court, the Hon.
" Robt. R. Livingston,[1] Chancellor of this State,

the first Constitution of the State; on the 8th May, 1777, was appointed one of the Puisne Judges of the Supreme Court; 23d October, 1779, was placed by the Legislature upon the Council to carry on the Government of the State in the Southern Portion thereof, during the Interval between the Enemy's Abandonment of the District and the Meeting of the Legislature. In 1788 he was a Member of the Convention which ratified the Constitution of the United States; on the 11th Jan., 1798, was appointed United States Senator to succeed Gen. Schuyler, and having attained the age of 60 resigned the Office of Judge of the New York Supreme Court, and also the same Year his Senatorship, on being appointed Judge of the United States District Court for New York; which Office he held at the Time of his Death, 4th Feb., 1805. (See Street's *Council of Revision*, p. 177.)

[1] ROBERT R. LIVINGSTON was born Nov. 27, 1747, and graduated at King's College, New York, in 1765. After completing his Law Studies with William Smith, he was appointed by Gov. Tryon, Recorder of the City; which Office he resigned at the beginning of the Revolution. In April, 1775, he was elected to the Assembly from Dutchess County. In 1776 · he

was a Member of Congress, and was placed on the Committee with Jefferson, Adams, Franklin, and Sherman, to whom was delegated the Task of Draughting the Declaration of Independence. He was also on other important Committees. In August, 1781, he was appointed Secretary for Foreign Affairs, and commenced his Duties October 20. The Foreign Business of Congress had previously been conducted by the Committee of Secret Correspondence. Domestick Affairs were also in part intrusted to him. He was diligent, prompt, and energetick. His valuable Correspondence has been published in the Diplomatick Correspondence edited by Jared Sparks. On his Resignation in 1783 he received the Thanks of Congress. Under the new Constitution of New York, which, as Chairman of the Committee, he assisted in forming, he was appointed Chancellor, and filled that Situation until 1801. In 1788 he was Chairman of the State Convention, which adopted the Federal Constitution; at that Time uniting his Efforts with those of Jay and Hamilton. In 1794 he declined the Appointment of Minister to France, offered by Washington. In 1801 he accepted the Office of Minister Plenipotentiary to France, and proceeded to Paris. He was received with respect by the First

" Mr. Platt, Mr. Wiſner, and Colonel Hathorn be,
" and hereby are, appointed Commiſſioners for the
" Purpoſe above mentioned, and proceed on that
" Buſineſs with all poſſible Deſpatch."[1]

This Committee reported, as follows :

" WEDNESDAY, Jan. 14, 1778.

" Your Committee, who were ſent to aſcertain
" the Place for fixing a Chain and erećting Forti-
" fications for Obſtrućting the Navigation of Hud-
" ſon's River, beg Leave to report : That they
" have carefully viewed the Ground on which Fort
" Clinton lately ſtood and its Environs, and find
" that the Ground is ſo interſećted with long deep
" Hollows, that the Enemy might approach with-
" out any Annoyance from the Garriſon within the
" Fort, to within a few Yards of the Walls, unleſs
" a Redoubt ſhould be raiſed to clear the Hollows
" next the Fort, which muſt be built at ſuch

Conſul, and after his Miſſion had cloſed, Napoleon preſented to him a ſplendid Snuff-Box, containing a Miniature of himſelf, by Iſabey. With the aſſiſtance of Mr. Monroe he made the very important Pur-chaſe of Louiſiana for $15,000,000. In Paris he formed an Intimacy with Robert Fulton, whom he aſſiſted by his Counſels and Money. After his Reſignation, and the Arrival of General Armſtrong, his Succeſſor, he travelled through Italy, Switzer-land, and Germany, and returned to America, in June, 1805. He died in 1813, aged 66. He was inſtrumental in the Introdućtion of Steam Navigation into the United States ; introduced the Merino Sheep, and the Uſe of Gypſum into New York ; was Preſident of an Agricultural Society ; and alſo Pre-ſident of the Academy of the Fine Arts. A more circumſtantial Ac-count of the Events of his Life is given in Street's *Council of Reviſion*, 149-59.

[1] Jour. Pro. Conv., 1113.

" Diſtance from the Fort that it could not be ſup-
" ported from thence in caſe of an Aſſault, ſo that
" the Enemy might make themſelves Maſters of
" the Redoubt the firſt Dark Night after their
" landing, which would be a good Work, ready to
" their Hand for annoying the Fort and facilitating
" their operations againſt it; and, together with
" the Eminences and broken Grounds within a
" ſhort Diſtance of the Fort, would render it im-
" poſſible for the Garriſon to reſiſt a general Aſ-
" ſault for many Hours together. Another objec-
" tion that appeared to the Committee was the
" want of Earth on the Spot, which would reduce
" the Engineer to the neceſſity of erecting his
" Works entirely of Timber, which muſt be
" brought to Pooploop's Kill in Rafts, and from
" thence drawn up a ſteep and difficult Road to the
" top of the Hill. The Rafts cannot be made till
" the Water is warm enough for Men to Work
" in it, by which it is probable that a Fort cannot
" be erected before the Ships of the Enemy will
" come up the River. Beſide, at this Place, the
" Chain muſt be laid acroſs the River ſo that it
" will receive the whole Force of the Ships coming
" with all the ſtrength of Tide and Wind, on a
" line of three or four miles. Add to theſe, if the
" Enemy ſhould be able to poſſeſs themſelves of the
" Paſſes in the Mountains through which they
" marched to the Attacks of Forts Montgomery
" and Clinton, it would be extremely difficult, if

R

" not impoſſible, for the Militia of the Country to
" raiſe the Siege.

" Upon viewing the Country at and about Weſt
" Point, the Committee found that there were
" ſeveral places at which the Enemy might land
" and proceed immediately to ſome high Grounds
" that would command a Fort erected at Weſt
" Point at the diſtance of ſix or ſeven hundred
" yards, from which they might carry on their ap-
" proaches through a light Gravelly Soil, ſo that it
" would be impoſſible for the Fort to ſtand a long
" Siege. But to balance this diſadvantage in this
" Place, there is plenty of Earth. The Timber
" may be brought to the Spot by good Roads from
" the high Grounds at the diſtance of one to three
" miles. Three hundred feet leſs of Chain will be
" requiſite at this Place than at Fort Clinton. It
" will be laid acroſs in a place where Veſſels going
" up the River moſt uſually loſe their Headway.[1]
" Water Batteries may be built on both ſides of the
" River for protecting the Chain and annoying the
" Ships coming up the River, which will be com-
" pletely commanded from the Walls of the Fort.
" There are ſo many Paſſes acroſs the Mountains
" to this Place, that it will be almoſt impoſſible

[1] Thoſe who are acquainted with the Place where the Obſtruction was faſtened to the Shore, will ſee the Force of this Deſcription. A Point of Land here juts out into the Stream abruptly and compels Veſ-ſels, ſailing under even the moſt favourable Breeze, to make ſuch Change in their Courſe as will ma-terially leſſen their Headway.

" for the Enemy to prevent the Militia from com-
" ing to the relief of the Garriſon.

" From theſe conſiderations, the Committee are
" led to conclude that the moſt Proper place to
" obſtruct the Navigation of the River is at Weſt
" Point;[1] but are at the ſame Time fully con-
" vinced that no Obſtructions on the banks of the
" River can effectually ſecure the Country, unleſs
" a Body of light Troops, to conſiſt of at leaſt two
" thouſand effective Men, be conſtantly ſtationed
" in the Mountains while the Navigation of the
" River is practicable, to Obſtruct the Enemy in
" their approach by Land.

" JNO. SLOSS HOBART,
" HENRY WISNER,
" JOHN HATHORN,
" ZEPH. PLATT.

" POUGHKEEPSIE, Jan. 14th, 1778."[2]

By Direction of Gen. Putnam, Hugh Hughes,
D. Q. M. G., viſited the Sterling Iron Works[3] of
Noble & Townſend, on the 2d of February, and

[1] In Force's *American Archievs,* Plans prepared by Bernard Romans are publiſhed, by which it will be ſeen that he firſt propoſed fortify- ing Weſt Point. His Plans, how- ever, were not carried out at that Time, Forts Clinton and Montgo- mery having been completed in- ſtead. The Plates in the *Archives,* therefore, have no value as deſcrib- ing the Forts at Weſt Point.

[2] Journ. Prov. Con. 1117.

[3] The Sterling Iron Works are ſtill in Operation. They are ſi- tuated on the Outlet of Sterling Pond, about five miles Southweſt of the Sloatſburgh Station, on the Erie Railway. They are owned by De- ſcendants of Peter Townſend, and have now been in Operation about one hundred Years.

entered into a Contract with the Proprietors to
Conftruct a Chain. This Contract was as follows :

" Articles of Agreement between Noble, Town-
" fend & Company, Proprietors of the Sterling
" Iron Works, in the State of New York, of the
" one Part, and Hugh Hughes, D. Q. M. G. to
" the Army of the United States, of the other
" Part, witneffeth :

" That the faid Noble, Townfend & Company,
" jointly and feverally engage to have made and
" ready to be delivered at their Works to the faid
" Hugh Hughes, D. Q. M. G. or to the D. Q.
" M. G. of the Middle Department for the Time
" being, on or before the firft Day of April next
" enfuing the Date hereof, or as much fooner as
" circumftances will admit, an Iron Chain of the
" following Dimenfions and Quality, that is, in
" Length five hundred yards—each Link about
" two feet long, to be made of the beft Sterling
" Iron, two inches and one quarter fquare, or as
" near thereto as poffible, with a Swivel to every
" hundred feet, and a Clevis to every thoufand feet,
" in the fame manner as thofe of the former Chain.

" The faid Noble, Townfend & Company alfo
" engage to have made and ready to be delivered
" at leaft twelve tons of Anchors of the aforefaid
" Iron, and of fuch Sizes as the faid Hugh Hughes
" or his Succeffors in Office fhall direct, in writ-

" ing, as ſoon as the completion of the Chain will
" admit.

" In Conſideration of which the ſaid Hugh
" Hughes, in behalf of the United States, agrees to
" pay to the ſaid Noble, Townſend & Company,
" or their Order, at the Rate of four hundred and
" forty Pounds for every ton weight of Chain[1] and
" Anchors delivered as before mentioned, unleſs
" the General Regulations on Trade, Proviſions,
" &c., which are now ſuppoſed to be framed by
" Deputies from the United States ſhall be publiſh-
" ed and take effect before the expiration of four
" Months from the date of this ; in which caſe
" the price is to be only £400 per ton for the ſaid
" Chain and Anchors. The Payment, if de-
" manded, to be made in ſuch proportion as the
" Work ſhall be ready to be delivered, which ſhall
" be determined in ten Days after requiſition made
" by a number of competent Judges, not leſs than
" three nor more than five, unconcerned with the
" Proprietors, or the Works, and if condemned, to
" be completed at the expenſe of the ſaid Com-
" pany, who are alſo to Repair, as aforeſaid, all
" failures of their Work, whenever happening,
" whether at the Works or River, or in extending
" it acroſs.

" The ſaid Hugh Hughes alſo engages to pro-
" cure of the Governor of this State, for the ſaid

[1] Continental Money probably.

" Noble, Townſend & Company, an exemptioñ
" for nine Months from the Date hereof, from
" Military Duty, for ſixty Artificers that are ſteadily
" Employed at the ſaid Chain and Anchors, till
" completed. Agreeable to the ſaid Exemption,
" the ſaid Company complying with the Terms
" thereof; Providing alſo that the ſaid Company
" give the ſaid Hugh Hughes, or his Succeſſors in
" Office, the Refuſal, by Letter, of all the Bar
" Iron, Anchors, &c., made at the ſaid Works in
" the ſaid Term of nine Months, at the current
" Price, unleſs what is neceſſary to Exchange for
" Clothing and other Articles for the Uſe of the
" Works.

" It is alſo Agreed, by the ſaid Parties, that if
" the Teams of the ſaid Company ſhall tranſport
" the ſaid Chain or Anchors, or any Part thereof,
" to any aſſigned Poſt, they ſhall receive for ſuch
" Services the ſame Pay as ſhall be given by the
" United States for the like; the Teams of the
" Company being exempted from Impreſs by any
" of the Q. M. G's Deputies during the ſpace of
" nine Months.

" Laſtly, the ſaid Company engage to Uſe their
" utmoſt endeavors to keep ſeven Fires at Forging
" and ten at Welding, if aſſiſted with ſuch Hands
" as are neceſſary and can be ſpared from the Army,
" in caſe of their not being able to procure others,
" the ſaid Company making deduĉtion for their
" Labor.

" In Witneſs whereof, the Parties have inter-
" changeably Subſcribed their Names this ſecond
" Day of February, one thouſand ſeven hundred
" and ſeventy-eight, and in the ſecond Year of
" American Independence.

" PETER TOWNSEND,
" In Behalf of Noble & Company.
" HUGH HUGHES,
" In Behalf of United States.

" In Preſence of ⎫
" P. TILLINGHAST." ⎭ [1]

On the 13th of February, Gen. Putnam wrote
to the Commander-in-Chief as follows:

" At my Requeſt the Legiſlature of this State
" have appointed a Committee to affix the Places
" and manner of ſecuring the River, and to afford
" ſome Affiſtance in expediting the Work. The
" State of Affairs now at this Poſt, you will obſerve
" is as follows : The Chain and neceſſary Anchor
" are Contracted for, to be completed by the firſt
" of April; and from the Intelligence I have re-
" ceived, I have reaſon to believe they will be
" completed by that Time. *Parts of the Boom in-*
" *tended to have been uſed at Fort Montgomery,*
" ſufficient for this Place are remaining. Some of
" the Iron is exceedingly bad, this I hope to have

---

[1] Copy of Original in Clinton Papers, State Library.

" replaced with good Iron foon.[1] The *Chevaux-*
" *de-Frize* will be completed by the Time the
" River will admit of finking them (Pollopel's
" Ifland). The Batteries near the Water, and the
" Fort to cover them, are laid out. The latter is
" within the Walls fix hundred yards around,
" twenty-one feet bafe, fourteen feet high, the
" *Talus* two inches to the foot. This I fear is too
" large to be completed by the Time expected.
" Governor Clinton and the Committee have
" agreed to this Plan, and nothing on my Part
" fhall be wanted to complete it in the beft and
" moft expeditious manner. Barracks and Huts
" for about three hundred Men are completed, and
" Barracks for about the fame number are nearly
" covered. A Road to the River has been made
" with great difficulty."[2]

Having proceeded thus far, Gen. Putnam went
to Connecticut, leaving Gen. Parfons in command ;
but, in the Abfence of explicit Authority, the latter, at firft, declined exercifing any thing more
than a mere Supervifory Power over the Works,
and little Progrefs was made. Meanwhile the
People of the Province, regarding the Works as

---

[1] By Reference to the Minutes
of the Secret Committee of July
14, the Character of the Boom referred to will be explained. The
whole Work and Plan, however,
was changed by Capt. Machin.
The Length of the Logs was reduced, fo that each Log of the
firft Boom made three of the new,
and the whole Arrangement of
Chains altered, as will appear in a
fubfequent Part of this Article.

[2] Sparks, v, 225..

really under Putnam's Command, became greatly incenſed at the Delay,[1] and refuſed to render the neceſſary Affiſtance while he remained, even nominally, at the Head of the Department. Indeed, the Current of Publick Opinion[2] ran ſo ſtrongly againſt Putnam that Waſhington appointed Gen. McDougall to repair to the Highlands and aſſume the Chief Command there, comprehending " the " Forts among other Objects of his Truſt."

Radière,[3] the Engineer, too, feeling ſome Delicacy in puſhing forward the Works in the irreſponſible State of the Command, viſited Congreſs, and reſigned his Appointment. He was ſucceeded

---

[1] The Courſe purſued by Gen. Parſons has been made the Subject of Cenſure in ſeveral of our Hiſtories, but, it is thought, very unjuſtly. (See Letters in Appendix.)

[2] PUTNAM ſuffered much in the Eſtimation of Reſidents in the Vicinity of Forts Clinton and Montgomery, and eſpecially of thoſe engaged in their Defence, for his Failure to render Affiſtance in Time to defeat Sir Henry Clinton. The old Story handed down from the Militiamen engaged in that Affair is, that Putnam was buſily engaged in a Game of Cheſs with a beautiful Lady, who was a Tory in Feeling; and that when warned of the Expedition, he refuſed to leave the Game until it was too late. This Story added greatly to his Diſcredit.

[3] LA RADIÈRE was one of four Engineers ſent over from France by Franklin and Deane, and was employed by Order of Congreſs. He was oppoſed to the Erection of Fortifications at Weſt Point, but was overruled by the unanimous Judgment of other Officers conſulted on the Occaſion, and Koſciuſzko was appointed to ſucceed him. (Loſſing's *Field Book*, 1, 704.) Mons. de la Radière was appointed Lieut. Col. of Engineers 8th July, 1777, in Accordance with a Treaty made in France, 13th Feb. 1777; was promoted to the Rank of Colonel 17th Nov. 1777; retained in the Service 1ſt Jan. 1779; died in Service ſame Year; Benefits of the Reſolution 10th April, 1780, extended to his Repreſentatives 3d Auguſt, 1785. *(Journals Congreſs.)*

S

by Kofciufko, who arrived at the Works on the 26th March,[1] Gen. McDougall arrived, on the 28th of the fame Month, and took Command. Operations were at once refumed and pufhed forward with Vigour.[2]

The Obftructions to the Navigation of the River, however, had fuffered lefs Delay than the Forts. Gov. Clinton, in Accordance with his Promife to " render any Affiftance in his Power," had exercifed confiderable Supervifion over that Branch of the Service; and had directed Capt. Machin, who had been employed in completing the Obftructions at Pollopel's Ifland, to take Charge of the Obftructions at Weft Point alfo.[3] The Links of the Chain were brought from the Sterling Iron

[1] " Mr. Kofciufko," fays Gen. McDougall, in a Letter dated April 13, " is efteemed by thofe who have attended the Works at Weft Point, to have more Practice than Col. Radière, and his Manner of treating the People is more acceptable than that of the latter; which induced Gen. Parfons and Gov. Clinton to defire the former may be continued at Weft Point."

[2] On the Recommendation of Gen. Wafhington, Congrefs decided, on the 31ft March, that all the Troops in the State of New York, fhould be under one General Officer who fhould be authorized to concentrate the whole Force in the Highlands until fuch Time as the Fortifications and Obftructions fhould be out of Danger of any fudden Attempt from the Enemy.

[3] Gov. Clinton, under Date of Feb. 13, 1778, thus certifies to Capt. Machin's Services: " I have Reafon to believe, that upon his Recovery (from Wounds received at Fort Montgomery), he has been fteadily engaged to this Time in the neceffary Preparations for fixing the new Chain acrofs the River, completing the Boom, the *Chevaux-de-Frize* (at Pollopel's Ifland), and in raifing the Galley (the Wafhington) which was funk (in Efopus Creek) on the Enemy's Advance up the River."

Works to Capt. Machin's Forges at New Windſor, where they were joined together and properly
faſtened to the Logs which formed the Support of
the Chain when completed.

I. From the Faɛts ſtated, it is apparent that the
Obſtruɛtions at Weſt Point conſiſted of a Boom
and a Chain. The former we find frequently referred to in the Papers quoted; and from the Portion of it which was recovered from the River by
Biſhop's Derrick, in the Summer of 1855, and
which is now depoſited in Waſhington's Head
Quarters, at Newburgh, a ſatisfaɛtory Deſcription
of it can be made.
The Relick here
referred to conſiſts
of two Logs, one
of White Wood and the other of White Pine,
about fifteen feet in length, and about twelve inches
in Diameter, dreſſed in the Center in the Form
of an Oɛtagon, and rounded at the Ends. Theſe
Logs are united to each other by an Iron Band
around each End and two Links of Chain of
nearly two inch Bar Iron, but which have evidently loſt much of their original Size from Corroſion.
This Boom extended the whole Width of the River,
in Front of the Chain. The Plan of its Conſtruction is repreſented by the following Engraving:

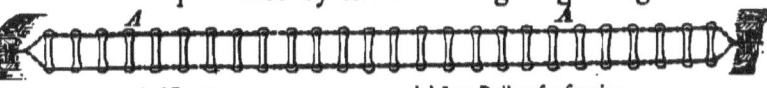

A A Boom.   *b b* Iron Rollers for ſecuring

It will be obferved, that the Boom combined great Strength[1] with Practicability.   It was, indeed,

[1] The Strength of this Boom may be inferred from the Bill of Noble & Townfend, which fpecifies 135 tons wrought into Booms, Bolts, Clips, Chains, Swivels and Bands, the very Articles of which the Relicks are compofed which were recovered, and, it is found, charged feparately from the Items which compofed the Chain. Its Conftruction was evidently commenced with the Intention of employing it at Fort Montgomery, as a Subftitute for the Rafts of Timber which were placed in Front of the Chain at that Place. (See Letter of General Putnam, *ante.)* The annexed Bill of Noble, Townfend & Co., it will be feen, commences before the Reduction of Fort Montgomery, and clofes before the Contract was made for the Chain. By the Bill of Capt. Machin, which is alfo annexed, it will be obferved that he calls the Boom *Chain Logs,* and that they were taken to Weft Point on that Day, April 7.   The Chain ("all fixed," fee his Letter) appears from the fame Bill to have been taken down on the 16th April, and ftretched acrofs the River on the 30th.

Quarter Mafter General by Meffieurs THOMAS MACHIN *and* JOHN NICOLL.

To NOBLE AND TOWNSEND Dr.

1777.	No. Clips.	No. Chains	No. Swivels.	No. Clevises.	No. Bolts.	No. Bands.	By whom fent.
Aug. 6.	24		6		24		Daniel McCoun.
" 21.	24		6		24		Francis Welding.
" "	20		5		20		Amos Mills.
" 23.			3	6	6	6	Francis Welding,
Sept. 2.	16	8			16		David Sutherland.
" 6.	12	6			12		D. McCoun as far as Thorn's.
" 17.	12	8			12		Partrick Sutherland.
" 25.	12	9			12	2	David Sutherland.
Oct. 2.		9					Daniel McCoun.
Nov.13.	22		1	1	22		Solomon Curtis.
Still at Works.		18			36		And one Lod was fent by the Clove that I have not
	142	58	21	7	184	8	got the Number Clips, &c.

the *Main Obstruction*, and was placed in Front of the Chain to receive the full Force of approaching Vessels.

The Wt is 17 Tuns, 10 C., 1 Qr. of Boome Iron, &c., at   £   *s. d.*

					£	s	d
140s, · ·	·	· · · ·	·	· · · · · · · 2453		1	3
To Making 29,249 lb. Clips, Chains, &c., at 1s 3d, ·	-	2453	1	3
June 19. To 20 0 0 Bar Iron by my Team at 140s,		140	0	0
" 24. " 30 0 14 do do at 140s,		210	17	6
" 26. " 20 0 4 do Col. Curlies at 140s, -		140	5	0
July 7. " 20 0 0 do our Team at 140s, ·		140	0	0
" " " 8 0 14 do Sam. Bruster, at 140s, -		56	17	6
1778.				
Jan. 20. " 10 0 14 do by Mandeville, at 330s,		167	1	3
" 28. " 10 1 14 do do do		171	3	4
" Carting 78 of the Boome Bar Iron, · · ·		12	16	0

£5945 3 1

			£	s	d
Augt. By Cash paid Mr. Hawxhurst,[1] - · £500 0 0				
Sept. 14. By Cash, - - - - - - - -	1000 0 0			
Nov. 14. By Cash paid Nathaniel Satly, · -	240 0 0			
Feb. 2. By Cash received by Col. Hughes,	4027 0 0			

5747 0 0

Ballance due, - - - - - - £198 3 1

The United States of America To THOMAS MACHIN *Dr. for Travelling Expenses and Money paid out in their service from January* 1778 *to Sept.* 20 *Agreeable to the Acount here under.*   £   *s. d.*
1778. Jan. 1. Exploring Hudsons River with 7 Men six Days,   6 10 0

---

1 WILLIAM HAWXHURST was a Hardware Merchant, doing Business in the City of New York. Peter Townsend of the Sterling Works married his Daughter. We infer from the following Letter, which is copied verbatim from the Original, that he was not much indebted to the Schoolmaster for any thing in his Line; but, in those Days, bad Spelling was not so much the Exception, as it is at present:

"SCOTS TAVERN, 23d April, 1778.
"SIR : I am Jurst now from Nobels at "Sterling. The Chane is going on fast. "But the anchors (not) Owing (They "say) to your Not Sending The wate of "Them. I Hope you will forward your "instructions on The Receipt of This, as "There Cant be any Thing Don Till you "Send The wate of Each pertickeler "anchor. I am Yours Sir in Haft,
                    "WM. HAWXHURST.
" To Cp. Machen, Indian Eare."

II. The Chain employed for Obstructing the River is amply described in the Contract with Noble & Townsend, already quoted, and by the

Jany 7.	Expences to PoughKeepse, - - - - - - -	1 10	6
do 12.	Expences at FishKill four Days Detayned on the publick service, - - - - - - - - -	4 0	0
do 16.	Expences on the Road to Chester to agree for the New Chain 3 Days, - - - - - - - -	3 12	6
do 20.	Expences Getting Timber for the Chain four Days,	4 0	0
do 26.	Getting up Drift Timber, - - - - - - - -	1 0	0
Feby 2.	Expences to New Burgh, New Malbrough and New Paltz 4 Days, - - - - - - - -	4 4	6
do 2.	For Ten Quire of Paper, - - - - - - -	2 10	0
do 12.	Expences to New Paltz 3 Days, Hiring one Hand two Days, - - - - - - - - -	4 10	6
do 17.	Expences to West Point, - - - - - - -	0 12	6
do 24.	Expences when in persute of Diserters, for Myself and Men, at McDonelds, - - - - - -	0 6	0
do	at Capt. Smiths, - - - - - - - - - -	4 8	0
do	at Sidmans, - - - - - - - - - - -	5 10	0
do	paid Onderdunk to Carry a Letter, - - - - -	1 12	0
March 5.	Getting the Logs to Drye for the Chain at New Paltz, - - - - - - - - - - -	3 10	0
do 11.	Expences to Jews Creek, Plattor Kill and New Burgh, two Days, - - - - - - - -	2 0	0
do 14.	Expences to West Pt, - - - - - - - -	0 12	0
do 15.	Expences from West Pt, - - - - - - -	0 12	0
do 16.	Expences to FishKill, PoughKeepse, New Paltz and New Malbrough, six Days, - - - - - -	6 0	0
do 24.	Expences to FishKill for Rigging, - - - - -	0 10	0
do 26.	Expences Down the High Lands Collecting Drift Timber, - - - - - - - - - -	0 12	6
do 29.	Expences to West Pt, - - - - - - - -	0 8	0
April 7.	Expences Getting Down the Chain Logs with 40 Men, 4 Days, - - - - - - - - -	6 0	0
do 12.	Expences to Chester, - - - - - - - -	1 0	0
do 16.	Taking Down the Chain, - - - - - - -	0 16	0
do 19.	Expences to Jews Creek, - - - - - - -	0 10	0
do 26.	Expences to Sterling, - - - - - - - -	1 10	6

Portion now preſerved at Weſt Point. For buoying the Chain, a large Quantity of Timber was
uſed, as appears from the following Extracts from
Capt. Machin's Papers:

" Jan. 20, 1778—Expenſes getting *Timber for*
" *the Chain*, four Days."

" Feb. 22d, 1778—We ſhall want a large quan-
" tity of *Timber for the Chain*, which cannot be
" got up the River on account of the Froſt and
" when the Froſt breaks up it will be to late for
" our Buſineſs."

		£	s	d
April 30.	While Getting the New Chain acrofs,	0	11	0
May 3.	Expences when Reafcending the Lady Wafhington Galley at Kingfton Creek, 20 Days,	9	10	6
June 1.	Expences to Peeks Kill,	1	11	0
do 4.	Expences to PoughKeepfe,	2	0	0
do 6.	Expences to FifhKill,	0	12	0
do 10.	Expences to Kingfton,	4	0	0
do 19.	Expences to Peeks Kill with four men,	2	0	0
do 24.	Expences to FifhKill with Ferrys,	1	12	6
do 29.	Expences to Pough Keepfe and Ferrys,	2	10	0
July 2.	Expences to FifhKill,	0	10	8
do 10.	Expences to Pough Keepfe and Ferrys with four men,	8	16	0
do 19.	Expences to Chefter,	1	0	6
do 20.	Expences to Fifh Kill,	0	11	0
Augt 1.	John Buchanons Bill for Travilling Expences,	5	1	0
do 2.	William McBrides Bill for Travilling Expences in the Service of the States,	5	4	0
	Jofeph Holfteads Bill for Travelling Expences in the Service of the States,	3	6	4
do 7.	Expences to Pough Keepfe,	2	0	0
do 20	Expences to Fifh Kill,	0	12	0
do	Expences tq Wit Plains,	6	0	0

£126 1 6

"March 5th, 1778—Getting the *Logs to dry*
"*for the Chain.*"

The Chain was put together at New Windſor;
floated down to Weſt Point, and ſecured in its proper Place in the latter Part of April, 1778, as appears from the following Extract from a Letter
from Gen. Clinton to Capt. Machin, dated
Poughkeepſie, 3 May, 1778:

"DEAR SIR:
"I received your Letter and am happy to
"learn that the Chain is acroſs the River, and that
"you had the good Fortune to accompliſh it ſo
"expeditiouſly and ſo much to your ſatisfaction."

The Chain, as it appeared when placed in its
Poſition, is thus deſcribed by Doctor Thacher in
his Journal:

"It is buoyed up by very large Logs of about
"ſixteen feet long, pointed at the Ends, to leſſen
"their oppoſition to the Force of the Current at
"Flood and Ebb Tide. The Logs are placed at
"ſhort diſtances from each other, the Chain carried
"over them and made faſt to each by Staples."

A great Variety of Traditions have been repeat-
ed, hiſtorically, in reference to the Obſtructions at
Weſt Point, and which may be fully explained
when the preciſe Character of the latter is underſtood. For Example, Mr. Loſſing, in his *Field
Book of the Revolution*, ſays:

" He [Arnold] wrote a Letter to Andre, in a
" diſguiſed Hand and Manner, informing him that
" he had weakened the Obſtructions in the River
" by ordering a Link of the Chain to be taken out
" and carried to the Smiths, under a pretenſe that
" it needed Repairs. He aſſured his Employer
" that the Link would not be returned to its Place
" before the Forts ſhould be in Poſſeſſion of the
" Enemy."

Arnold could not have taken a Link from the
Chain without removing that Part of the Obſtructions altogether; but he could eaſily have weakened
the *Boom* by removing a Link from either Side,
Again, Mr. Simms, in a recent Letter to the Albany *Argus,* ſays:

" Gov. Clinton is ſaid, with Others, to have
" *walked acroſs the River on the Chain;* and an
" old Gentleman by the Name of Wood, who a
" few Years ago was living at Springfield, Otſego
" County, aſſured me that *he* had croſſed the River
" *on the Chain.*"

Theſe Traditions are eaſily reconciled by ſubſti-
tuting the Word *Boom* for that of *Chain.* The *Boom*
could be readily converted into a Bridge; and it is not
improbable that in its Conſtruction, Reference was
had to this Object, as it would afford Facilities for
the tranſport of Troops from one Side of the River
to the Other, the Abſence of which had Contribut-

T

ed ſo much to the Loſs of Forts Clinton and
Montgomery. Another Writer affirms, that the
Chain was removed every Winter " by means of a
" large Windlaſs," and that it made a " huge Pile
" on the River Bank." The ſimple faɛt in reference to this is, that one End of the Chain and of
the Boom being looſened from its Faſtening, a
Windlaſs was employed to ſwing the Body around
to the Shore, a very ſimple Proceſs and eaſily accompliſhed.

But we will not purſue this Branch of the Sub-
jeɛt farther. A large Portion of the Chain was
ſold to the Weſt Point Foundry at Cold Spring,
many Years ago, where it was worked up. In
removing the *Boom* finally, a portion of it became
detached, and the Logs being Water-ſoaked, ſunk
to the Bottom of the River, whence after being
waſhed by the Tide for over eighty Years, they
have been recovered; and now ſerve the noble
Purpoſe of elucidating an important Branch in the
defenſive Operations of the Province of New York
in the Struggle for Independence.

Relick of Chain preſerved at Weſt Point.

VI.

B E A C O N S

A N D

S I G N A L S .

THE

B E A C O N S

AND

S I G N A L S .

EACONS were the rude Telegraphs
of former Centuries, and were no
unimportant Part of the Machinery
employed in this Conteſt. In our
Hiſtories are many Alluſions to the
Beacon-Hills of the Highlands; Tradition
alfo has handed down many Tales of the
" Alarm-Fires that often gleamed on their
Summits during the War." So far as we
have read, however, nothing really tangible
has ever been publiſhed on the Subjeᴄt. Revelling
among the old Manuſcripts at Head Quarters, we
have found a few Items touching the Signals which
were employed during the Revolution for convey-

ing Intelligence of the Approach of the Enemy and
to direct the Movements of the Militia and Continental Forces, which we have thought of sufficient
Interest to warrant their Publication in a durable
Form.

On the 7th of October, 1775, the Continental
Congress suggested to the Provincial Congress of
New York the expediency of Adopting, in Connec-
tion with the Colonies of Connecticut and New
Jersey, Signals for conveying Intelligence. The
Resolution of the Continental Congress was as fol-
lows :

" *Resolved*, That it be recommended to said
" Convention to Establish, at proper Distances,
" Posts to be ready to give Intelligence to the
" Country, in case of any Invasion, or by Signals to
" give Alarms in case of Danger ; and that they
" confer with the Assembly of Connecticut and the
" Convention of New Jersey, on the speediest
" Manner of conveying Intelligence in such Cases
" and receiving Assistance when necessary."

In accordance with this Suggestion, the Provincial Congress of New York, on the 17th of Oct.,
1775, adopted the following :

" *Resolved*, That in Order to give a General
" Alarm throughout the Colony in case of Inva-
" sion, and for the purpose of mustering the Regi-
" ments aforesaid (Minute Men), that Beacons be

" erected at convenient Places and Diftances
" throughout the Colony; and where convenient
" Places cannot be found to erect Beacons, that
" Cannon be fixed inftead of them, and that fome
" fit Perfon be employod under the Direction and
" with the Advice of the feveral County Commit-
" tees, to make a proper Arrangement for this Bufi-
" nefs, and to report thereon to the Congrefs.

" And for the purpofe of conveying Intelligence
" in cafe of Invafion, that it be recommended to
" the feveral County Committees in this Colony,
" to appoint and engage fome one or more of their
" own Body (whofe Place of Refidence fhall be
" convenient for the Purpofe, or any other difcreet
" Perfon or Perfons who fhall live on or near the
" moft Public Roads that lead from New York
" through their refpective Counties), to have a
" Perfon and Horfe in readinefs to forward Intelli-
" gence in cafe of Invafions, and that the Commit-
" tees fix the feveral Stages in their refpective
" Counties from 10 to 15 miles Diftance."

A Copy of the Refolution of the Continental
Congrefs and alfo the Refolutions of the Provincial
Congrefs were forwarded to the Aflembly of Connecticut and the Provincial Congrefs of New Jerfey, " together with a Letter requefting their
" Advice on the Subject." A Letter was alfo ordered to the Colonels of Militia and Minute Men,
ftating that, " In order that timely Affiftance may

" be had in cafe of an Invafion on this Colony,
" Directions will be given by the Congrefs for the
" Erection of Beacons at fome and Cannon in other
" Places of the Colony to alarm the Country.
" Thefe Signals, when erected, will be fo arranged
" as to prevent any Miftakes in the Alarm." In
reply to the Letter from the Congrefs of New
York, Governor Trumbull, of Connecticut ref-
ponded : " Your Plan is approved by the Council
" of Safety, and I am requefted by them to procure
" proper Perfons to be in readinefs at a Minute's
" Warning to carry any Intelligence of Alarm or
" Invafion to the Towns where Occafion may re-
" quire."

This Plan was immediately carried into Effect,
as appears from the following Paper enclofed by
Gov. Tryon[1] to the Earl of Dartmouth, under Date
of Nov. 11th, 1775, viz :

[1] WILLIAM TRYON received a Commiffion as Lieutenant and Captain of the 1ft Regiment of Foot Guards 12th October, 1751 *(Army Lifts)*; in 1757 married Mifs Wake, of Hanover Street, with whom he received a Fortune of £20,000 Sterling *(Gentleman's Magazine,* xxvii, 577), and on 30th September, 1758, became Captain and Lieutenant Colonel in the Guards. Through fome Court Influence probably, (as we find a Mifs Tryon Maid of Honor to the Queen *(Ib.* xxxi, 431), and he claimed Relationfhip with the Raw- don or Moira Family), he was appointed Lieutenant Governor of North Carolina, where he arrived 27th October, 1764, and, on the Death of Mr. Dobbs, was gazetted Governor of that Colony 20th July, 1765. *(Ib.* xxxv, 347). He adminiftered that Government until July, 1771, when he was advanced to that of New York. He was promoted to a Colonelcy in the Army 25th May, 1772; became Third Major of the Guards 8th June, 1775; Major General 29th Auguft, 1777, and Colonel of the 70th Regiment 14th May, 1778.

" Hancock's Letter to the Congrefs, fays, ' I alfo
" enclofe, you a Refolve of the Continental Con-
" grefs refpecting thofe who in your Opinion are
" dangerous by going at Large, to which I alfo
" refer.' This Refolve I can't get fight of. I be-
" lieve it is deftroyed. 150 Men working at the
" Forts, 200 weight of Powder there. Beacons to
" be erected 30 miles this Side of the Forts all the
" Way up at proper Places to give the alarm. A
" Plan is laid to build two more Batteries this Side
" of the Forts. An Application to Congrefs for
" 25 Men to keep Watch at Night, at the Forts
" building up the North River. A Plan to fink
" Blocks to ftop up fome narrow Places going up
" to the Forts, in order to prevent large Veffels
" going up."[1]

In the Spring of 1776, Gen. Wafhington ad-

In 1779 his Name was inferted in the New York Act of Confifcation. It is unneceffary here to fpeak of his Career in America, as that is already Notorious as it was Odious. He refigned the Government, for many Years only Nominal, of New York 21ft March, 1780, and re-turned to England, where he was appointed Lieutenant General 20th November, 1782, and Colonel of the 29th Foot 16th Auguft, 1783. Governor Tryon died at his Houfe, Upper Grovefnor Street, London, 27th Jan. 1788, and his Remains were depofited in the Family Vault at Twickenham. A highly eulo-

giftick Obituary Notice of him, doubtlefs from the Pen of his Son-in-law Fanning, appeared fhortly after, in the *Gents. Mag.* LVIII, 179. " The Name of Tryon," it afferts, " will be revered acrofs the Atlan-" tick while Virtue and Senfibility " remain." The State of New York manifefted its Reverence foon after by erafing the Name of Tryon from the only County that bore his Name in the State. (*N. Y. Col. Hift.* VIII, 798.)

[1] New York Colonial Hiftory, VIII, 615.

U

dreſſed the Convention of New York on the Subject, communicating the Plan which Gens. Sullivan and Green, and Lord Stirling[1] had ſuggeſted to
him for conveying Intelligence of the Approach of
the Enemy's Fleet, and ſuggeſting that the Convention ſhould employ the ſame in calling in the
Militia under its Control. This Plan was as follows :

" To His Excellency Gen. Waſhington, Com-
" mander-in-Chief of the American Army :
" May it pleaſe Your Excellency : In Obedience
" to the Orders given us, we have met and deli-

<hr>

[1] WILLIAM ALEXANDER, generally
ſtyled, through Courteſy, *Lord Stirling,* was born in New York City,
in 1726, but paſſed a Portion of
his Life in New Jerſey. He claimed
to be the rightful Heir to the Title
and Eſtates of the Earldom of Stirling in Scotland, from which Country his Father came, though the
Government refuſed to acknowledge
the Son's Claim, when he repaired
to Great Britain in Purſuit of his
Inheritance. He was early remark-
able for his Fondneſs for Mathe-
maticks and Aſtronomy, in which
Sciences he made conſiderable Progreſs. He was Aid-de-Camp and
Private Secretary to Gov. Shirley in
the French War, was a Member of
the Provincial Council of New Jerſey, and on the Approach of the
Revolution was appointed to the
Command of a Regiment of Militia,
and ultimately roſe to the Rank of
Major-General. He acted an important Part throughout the War,
and diſtinguiſhed himſelf particularly in the Battles of Long Iſland,
Germantown, and Monmouth. In
the firſt he was taken Priſoner, after
having, by a bold Attack upon a
Corps commanded by Cornwallis,
effected the Eſcape of a large Part
of his Detachment. In the ſecond,
his Diviſion, with the Brigades of
Genls. Naſh and Maxwell, formed
the *Corps de Reſerve;* and in the
laſt, he commanded the Left Wing
of the American Army. He was
always warmly attached to Waſhington, and the Cauſe which he eſ-
pouſed. He died at Albany, N. Y.
15th Jan. 1783, aged 57, leaving
behind him the Reputation of a
brave, diſcerning and intrepid Officer, and a learned and honeſt Man.
His Biography has been written by
his Grandſon, W. A. Duer.

" berated upon the feveral Matters referred to us
" by Your Excellency, and beg leave to Report
" that the following Signals be given upon the Ap-
" proach of any number of Ships toward this Port
" (New York), viz :   Upon the Appearance of any
" Number of Ships by Day from one to fix, a large
" Flag is to be hoifted over the Highlands of
" Neverfink ; upon the Appearance of any Number
" from fix to twenty, two Flags; and for any
" greater number, three Flags; the Flags to be
" hoifted upon Flag-Staffs arranged there from
" eaft to weft at twenty Yards Diftance from each
" other.   The Signal by Night to be given by an
" equal number of Fires arranged in the fame Order
" and at the fame Places; thefe Signals to be re-
" peated both by Day and Night on the Heights
" of Staten Ifland by Flags and Fire arranged in
" the fame Manner.   The Commanding Officer
" in each of thofe Departments to fee that a good
" Look-out be kept for Ships both by Day and
" Night, and upon their Appearance he is not only
" to give the Signals before mentioned, but is as
" foon as poffible to give Intelligence by Exprefs
" to the Commander-in-Chief.

   " We recommend that the Day Signal be given
" by large Enfigns with broad Stripes of Red and
" White, and that upon the Appearance of three
" Flags by Day or three Fires by Night, the
" Country is to take the alarm and communicate it

" as foon as poffible, for the purpofe of calling in
" the Militia.

> " JNO. SULLIVAN.
> " NATHANIEL GREENE.
> " STIRLING."

To this Letter the Convention refponded that
" We have not been entirely inattentive to the Sub-
" ject of this Part of your Recommendation ; every
" Regiment of our Militia has its Place of Rendez-
" vous appointed, and Riders are fixed at the dif-
" ferent Stages in this and the neighboring Colo-
" nies, to alarm the Country in cafe of an Invafion ;
" but if upon confideration we fhall judge that
" Signals may be of Service in calling in our Mili-
" tia more fpeedily than can be done in that Way,
" we fhall communicate to you our own Determi-
" nation on that Head."

We find no further Mention of the Subject in the
Proceedings of the Provincial Convention. In
1777, Lord Stirling, commanding at Albany, with a
general Supervifion of Military Affairs between
that Place and New York, iffued an Order for the
Erection of Beacons and Alarm Pofts in Accordance
with the Plan which he had fuggefted to Wafhington in 1776, above quoted. Thefe Beacons
were erected on the Hills from the Frontier Pofts
in Weftchefter to Beacon-Hill, and from thence
diverged along the Hills eaft into Connecticut, and
fouth and weft through New Jerfey by way of

Morriſtown, Pluckemin and Middlebrook, and to
the Neverſink Hills at Sandy Hook. They con-
ſiſted of Flags and Alarm Cannon by Day, and
Fires and Alarm Cannon by Night; and were ſo
arranged as to exhibit the Point where an Attack
by the Enemy was expected. The following
Deſcription of the Manner in which the Beacon-
Fires were made was copied from Stirling's original
Order by Mr. Loſſing, and is given in his *Field
Book of the Revolution*, as follows:

" Each of the Beacons are to be of the follow-
" ing Dimenſions : at Bottom fourteen feet Square,
" to riſe in a pyramidal Form to about eighteen or
" twenty feet high, and then to terminate about
" ſix feet ſquare, with a ſtout Sapling in the Cen-
" tre of about thirty feet high from the Ground.
" In Order to erect them, the Officer who overſees
" the Execution ſhould proceed thus : he ſhould
" order the following ſized Logs to be cut as near
" the Place as poſſible; twenty Logs of fourteen
" feet long and about one foot Diameter; two Logs
" of about twelve feet long; ten Logs of about
" ten feet long; ten Logs of about nine feet long;
" ten Logs of about eight feet long; twenty Logs
" of about ſeven feet long; twenty Logs of about
" ſix feet long. He ſhould then ſort his longeſt
" Logs as to diameter, and place the four longeſt
" on the Ground parallel to each other and about
" three feet from each other. He ſhould then

" place the four next Logs in ſize acroſs theſe at
" Right Angles, and ſo proceed until all the Logs
" of fourteen feet be placed.   Then he is to go on
" in the ſame Manner with Logs of twelve feet
" long, and when they are all placed, with thoſe of
" a leſſer Size till the whole are placed, taking Care
" as he goes on to fill the Vacan-
" cies between the Logs with old
" dry ſplit Wood or uſeleſs dry
" Rails and Bruſh, not too cloſe,
" and leaving the fifth Tier open
" for Firing and Air.   In the be-
" ginning of his Work, to place
" a good ſtout Sapling in the
" Centre, with part of its Top
" left about ten or twelve feet
" above the whole Work.   The
" two upper Rows of Logs ſhould
" be faſtened in their Places with good ſtrong
" Wooden Plugs or Trunnels."

Here, then, were the Beacon-Fires which were
lighted upon Beacon Hill and Butter Hill,[1] at the
northern Entrance of the Highlands, and which
Tradition tells us were reſponded to by Beacons on

[1] *Beacon Hill,* in Dutcheſs
County near Fiſhkill, is 1685 feet
in height.   Butter Hill, the northern moſt Peak of the Highlands,
is in the Town of Newburgh,
Orange County, having an Altitude
of 1529 feet.   Mr. Willlis has en-
deavoured to change the Name of
this Eminence to *Storm King,*
which ſhould not be encouraged.
Names hallowed by Hiſtorick Aſſo-
ciation, however homely and un-
poetick they may be, ſhould not be
diſplaced by others of mere Fancy.

Mullender's Hill at Little Britain, and Snake Hill[1] juſt weſt of Newburgh, in the Vicinity of which Points the Militia and Portions of the Continental Troops were encamped.[2] As we have already ſtated, the Lighting of the Beacons was accompanied by the Diſcharge of Cannon. The following Copy of an Order iſſued by Gen. James Clinton, which was found among the Papers of Capt. Machin, by J. R. Simms, Eſq., and publiſhed in his *Hiſtory of Schoharie County*, ſhows the Manner of uſing the Beacons and the Alarm Cannon :

" HEAD QUARTERS,

" FORT MONTGOMERY, July 10th, 1777.

" The Signals to be given on the Approach of " the Enemy: On the firing of two Cannon at " Peekſkill, by Gen. Varnum[3] one Minute from

---

[1] *Snake Hill* is a rough, rocky Eminence in the northeaſt Part of New Windſor, Orange County, of about 600 feet Elevation above Tide Water. (French's *New York Gazetteer*, 509.)

[2] The Range of the Beacons in the Winter of 1779-80 may be aſcertained from the Location of the Continental Forces. Waſhington's Head Quarters were at White Plains ; ſeven Brigades were encamped at Middlebrook, N, J., nine Brigades on the weſt Bank of the Hudſon, from New Windſor to Shawangunk, ſix Brigades on the eaſt Bank of the River at Fiſhkill

and Vicinity, three Brigades at Danbury, Conn., and the Artillery at Pluckemin, N. J.

[3] JAMES MITCHELL VARNUM was born at Dracut, Maſs., 1749, and was graduated at Rhode Iſland College in 1769 ; was admitted to the Bar 1771, and ſettled at Eaſt Greenwich, R. I., in the practice of the Law ; entered the Army 1775, and commanded a Regiment at Bunker Hill ; was appointed Brigadier-General 1777 ; reſigned 1779, and was elected to Congreſs ſame Year, and again in 1786 ; was appointed Judge of the North Weſtern Territory 1787 ; died

" each other, two will be fired by Gen. Hunting-
" ton,[1] two by Gen. Parſons; to be anſwered by
" two at Fort Independence, two at Fort Mont-
" gomery, two at Fort Conſtitution, *and the Bea-*
" *con there to be fired as uſual;* to be anſwered by
" two from the braſs twenty-four Pounder near
" New Windſor.   Upon this Signal, the Militia on
" weſt Side of Hudſon's River, in the County of
" Orange and Ulſter, as far as Col. Haſbrouck's
" Regiment,[2] including the ſame, are to march by
" Detachments, without further Notice, as a Re-
" inforcement of this Garriſon, and the Militia on
" the eaſt Side of the River, as far up as Pough-

10th Jan., 1789, aged 40, termi-
nating a remarkably active but brief
Career. His Biography is ſketched
at length in Hildreth's *Settlers of
Ohio,* 165-85.

[1] Jedediah Huntington was
born in Norwich, Conn., 15th
Auguſt, 1743; was graduated
at Harvard 1763; entered the
Army as Colonel of a Regiment
1775; was appointed Brigadier
General May, 1777; was afterwards Aid to Waſhington; was
Member of the Court Martial
which tried Andre. After the
War was Sheriff of his native
County, and ſubſequently State
Treaſurer; and in 1789 was appointed Collector of the Port of
New London, which Office he held
until 1815, when he reſigned. He
died 25th Sept., 1818, aged 75.

[2] Jonathan Hasbrouck was a
Deſcendant of one of the firſt Hu-
guenot Settlers of the Paltz, Ulſter
County. He removed to Newburgh in 1753, and, in 1760, was
elected Superviſor on the Organ-
ization of the Town. At the
breaking out of the War, he commanded a Regiment of Ulſter
County Militia, which at a previous Date he reported as conſiſting
of 608, Officers included, divided
into 11 Companies; " likewiſe 450
" Firelocks, 293 Swords, 188 Car-
" tridge Boxes, 32 lbs Powder, and
" 120 lbs Lead. A true State of
" my Regiment after the fourth
" Man was ſelected as a Minute
" Man." His Place of Rendez-
vous in Caſe of Alarm was the
Houſe of Martin Wygond in Newburgh. *(Jour. Com. Safety.)*

" keepſie, including Col. Frew's Regiment, to
" march for the Reinforcing of the Garriſon under
" Gen. Putnam.

" This Order is immediately to be publiſhed by
" the Commanding Officer at Fort Conſtitution,
" and Copies of it tranſmitted by him to Capt.
" Lieut. Machin, of the Artillery at New Wind-
" ſor, that he may çauſe the ſame to be publiſhed
" there."

Of courſe there is no Reçord ſhowing when
theſe Signals gave their Warnings. They were
firſt uſed, probably, when the Engliſh made their
Approach on Forts Montgomery and Clinton, and
afterwards as the Movements of the Enemy rendered it neceſſary. In 1779, the Beacons were
diſcontinued, by Order of Gen. McDougall,[1] then

---

[1] ALEXANDER McDOUGALL, was, ſome ſay, a Native of Scotland; Allen ſays he was the Son of a Scotchman who ſold Milk in the City of New York, and that he was not aſhamed to acknowledge that, when a Boy, he aſſiſted his Father. He became early an ac- tive Member of the Body known as Sons of Liberty, and was arreſt- ed in February, 1770, on a Charge of being the Author of the *Addreſs to the Betrayed Inhabitants of New York,* and refuſing to give Bail, was committed to Priſon by Order of Chief Juſtice Horſmanden. His Friends repreſented his Caſe as ſimi- lar to that of Wilkes. The latter had brought down the Vengeance of Government by the Publication of the *North Briton,* No. 45. This Number became the Watçhword of McDougall's fellow Patriots, and when aſked their Names, on ſeek- ing Admiſſion to their Friend, their Anſwer was: "We are forty-five;" and ſaluted their Champion with "forty-five" Cheers. In the two Months of his Confinement, he was overrun with Viſitors. On the 20th of December following he was arraigned at the Bar of the Aſ- ſembly on the ſame Charge, on which Occaſion he was defended

V

in Command of the Forces in the Highlands, and the Alarm Guns and Exprefs Riders only employed. The original Order of Gen. Clinton, made in Compliance with that of Gen. McDougall, on this Point, is depoſited among the old Manuſcripts at Head Quarters, in Newburgh,[1] and is as follows :

by George Clinton, afterwards the firſt Governor of the State of New York. A Writ of Habeas Corpus was fued out in the Courſe of the following Month, but without any Reſult, and Mr. McDougall was not liberated from his Confinement until the 4th of March, 1771, when the Aſſembly was prorogued. In March, 1775, he was a Member of the Provincial Convention, and was nominated as one of the Candidates for the Continental Congreſs at Philadelphia, but was not elected; in the fame Year he received a Commiſſion as Colonel of the 1ſt New York Regiment. He roſe in 1776 to the Rank of Brigadier General, and in the following Year was preſent at the Battle of Germantown. In 1777 he was appointed Major General, and in 1778, fuperſeded Putnam in the Command of the Highlands. After the Flight of Arnold, he was put in Charge of Weſt Point on the 5th October, 1780. In the Year 1783, he was elected to repreſent the Southern Diſtrict in the New York Senate, and continued a Member of that Body until his Death, which occurred in June, 1786. At the Time of his Deceaſe, General Mc-

Dougall was Preſident of the Bank of New York, and in Politicks adhered to the Hamilton Party. *(Leake's Life of John Lamb; N. Y. Col. Hiſt.,* viii, 213.)

[1] Overlooking the Hudſon, in the ſouth Part of the Village of Newburgh, ſtands an old Stone Manſion known as Waſhington's Head Quarters. It is ſurrounded by a fine Lawn of ſeveral Acres; and the whole Premiſes are owned and kept in Order by the State. The Building was commenced by Burger Meynders, one of the firſt Settlers of the Town, who ſold it, in 1749, to Alex. Colden. Colden ſold it, in 1753, to Jonathan Haſbrouck, and in his Poſſeſſion and thoſe of his Deſcendants it remained for nearly a hundred Years, and from this Fact it became known as the Old Haſbrouck Houſe. Mr. Haſbrouck added the Kitchen on the ſouth in 1760, making it a long, narrow Building. In 1770 he added the whole length of the weſt Side, and a new Roof was thrown over the whole. There are 8 Rooms on the firſt Floor, and from the principal Room eight Doors open, leading to every Part of the Houſe, including

" POUGHKEESIE, March 18th, 1779.

" GENERAL ORDERS.—The Signal of Alarm
" being fixed by the Orders of the Honourable
" Major General McDougall, on the 19th Feb.
" laſt, are as follows, viz :

" When five Topſail Veſſels appear coming up
" of the Enemy, three Cannon will be fired at
" King's Ferry, five Minutes after each other ; and
" if ten Veſſels appear, four Cannon will be fired
" at the ſame Diſtance of Time, and in this Man-
" ner if a greater number of Ships appear, that is
" one Gun for every five that ſhall exceed that
" number. Theſe Signals will be anſwered by the
" firing of the heavieſt Cannon at Weſt Point in
" the ſame Manner.

" It is his Excellency the Governor's Orders
" that the ſame be Communicated to the Officers
" of the reſpective Regiments of Militia of the

the Chambers and Cellar, while it has but one Window. This Building was uſed by Waſhington for his Head Quarters while the American Army occupied this Poſition upon the Hudſon. It was purchaſed by the State in 1850, and is kept as nearly as poſſible in its original Condition. The Rooms and the Grounds are filled with Relicks of the Revolution and Mementos of the War of 1812 and the Mexican War. The Walls of the Bedroom occupied by Waſhington are covered by Original Letters of Waſhing-ton, La Fayette, and other diſtinguiſhed Men of the Revolution, framed and glazed. Among the Curioſities are the Tables uſed by Waſhington and La Fayette. Part of the Boom which was ſtretched acroſs the Hudſon, and a great variety of Warlike Implements. Near the northeaſt Corner of the Houſe is the Grave of Uzal Knapp, the laſt of Waſhington's Life Guard; he died in Jan., 1856. (French's *New York Gazetteer,* 509.)

" Counties of Duchefs, Ulfter and Orange, who are
" ftrictly charged to fee their men are properly
" provided with Arms and Amunition and held in
" the moft perfect Readinefs : and that upon the
" Alarms being given, Col. Commandant Swart-
" wout's Brigade will immediately march to Fifh-
" kill, and there wait further Orders, and the Re-
" giments of Ulfter and Orange (the Weftern
" Frontier Companies who are to attend to the
" Protection of the Frontier Settlements excepted),
" to the Poft at Weft Point.

" As the Signal Guns may not be heard but by
" the Regiments next contiguous to the Pofts, the
" Officers of thofe Regiments are to communicate
" it by exprefs to the other Regiments on their
" refpective Sides of the River.

" This is to be confidered as a Standing Order
" until reverfed; and as the Safety of the Country
" greatly depends on the fpirited exertions of the
" Militia to reinforce the Continental Troops and
" ftrengthen the different Pofts on fudden Emer-
" gencies it is expected that thefe Orders will be
" moft faithfully complied with.

" By Order of his Excellency
" Governor Clinton,
" Robt. Benson, A. D. C."

The following Letter from Gen. Heath, in reply to an Inquiry on the Subject by Gov. Clinton
(the Original of which is depofited at Head Quar-

ters in Newburgh), gives fome Additional light on the Subject:

" *To His Excellency Governor Clinton :*
         "HEAD QUARTERS,
      " Robinfon Houfe, Dec. 20th, 1779. }
   " SIR:
      " I have the honor to enclofe and forward " your Excellency a Letter received this Morning " by Exprefs from his Excellency Gen. Wafhing- " ton

      " I have not been able to give you a Statement " of the feveral Beacons, agreeable to your requeft " of the 2d inft., until now.   Upon enquiring, I " found that the Guard at the one on Butter Hill " had been taken off for fome Time.   I could not " find by whofe Order it was done until applica- " tion was made to Gen. McDougall, from whom " I learned that the Guard before mentioned was " taken off with the approbation of the Comman- " der-in-Chief.   As this Beacon muft give the " Signal to the others, the other Guards are ren- " dered of no Service.   I have, therefore, thought, " as it will be extremely difficult and uncomfort- " able to continue Guards on the Tops of thofe " Mountains where the Beacons are erected thro' " the fevere Seafon, and as there is little probability " of the Enemy making any confiderable move- " ments during that Time, that the Guards in " general had beft be taken off, if you coincide in

" Opinion with me; and that as ſoon as the Sea-
" ſon advances, when the Enemy may be appre-
" hended to be in Motion, the Guards ſhould be
" again mounted; or if any Intelligence before
" that Time ſhould indicate the Enemy to have
" Intentions this way, immediate Attention ſhould
" be paid to the Beacons. I cannot find, from any
" Intelligence yet obtained, that a Beacon was ever
" fixed at one of the Places you mention, viz: on
" Mullender's Hill in Little Britain.

" The Enemy undoubtedly are making a large
" Embarkation of Troops, if they have not already
" ſailed; it is ſaid at leaſt 10,000. Forrage and
" Fuel are exceedingly ſcarce with them.
" I have the honor to be
" With great reſpect,
" Your Excellency's moſt obt. Servt.,
" W. Heath."

It is probable that the Beacons were again employed in 1780, when important Movements were
made by both the Enemy and the Continental
Forces in the Vicinity of New York. We are
told, that Arnold, when diſcovered going down the
River in an open Boat, made the Excuſe to Waſhington for his Conduct, that his Object was to
" eſtabliſh Signals as near the Enemy's Lines as
" poſſible, by which he might receive Information
" of any Movements of a Fleet or Troops up the
" Hudſon." If ſuch was the Fact, how muſt thoſe

Signals have flafhed under the Hands of the ftern Patriots when his dark Treachery was difcovered. The whole Heavens glowed with the Infignia of Danger, and the Valleys rung with the reverberating Peals of Alarm Guns and the Clatter of the Hoofs of Exprefs Horfes, as Meffengers fped on their Way to rally the patriot Forces to the Defence of the Gibralter of the American Independence. From this Period, down to the Clofe of the War, comparative Tranquility refted around the Highlands ; and the Beacon Hills were dark. The laft gleaming Crowns which flafhed on their Brows proclaimed the TRIUMPH OF FREEDOM.

APPENDIX.

APPENDIX.

Page 104.

JAMES DUANE

WAS born in the City of New York, 6th Feb., 1732-3, and adopted the Profeſſion of the Law, which he ſtudied with James Alexander, the Father of Lord Stirling. On the 21ſt Oct., 1759, he married a Daughter of Col. Robert Livingſton. His Father left him a large Eſtate in Duaneſburgh, Schenectady County, N. Y., which he increaſed by Purchaſes until he owned nearly the whole of that Townſhip, and began its Settlement by a Company of Germans, in 1765. About the ſame Time he became the Owner of ſixty-four thouſand Acres of Land in Vermont. He was a Member of moſt of the Committees in the City of New York raiſed to deviſe Plans of oppoſing the Britiſh Encroachments, and was elected a Member of the firſt Congreſs. He ſet out for Philadelphia, 31ſt Auguſt, 1774, accompanied from his Houſe to the Ferry by a great Proceſſion; with Muſick and Banners. The Congreſs adjourned on the 26th October, and the New York Delegates paid their own Expenſes. In April, 1775, he was elected a Member to the ſecond Congreſs. During the Receſs of Congreſs, in Auguſt, he attended the Indian Treaty at Albany. He continued in Congreſs until 31ſt May, 1776, when he was called Home to attend the New York Congreſs. He took his Seat in that Body 2d June, but left New York on the 6th, having obtained leave of Abſence to procure a Place of Reſidence for his Family; and did not again ſet his Foot in his native City until he entered it in Triumph, 25th November, 1783. The Convention alſo retired on the Invaſion of the Britiſh Troops, and aſſembled at Fiſhkill, where Mr. Duane joined it on the 1ſt Auguſt. He was ſent on the ſame Day, as one of a Committee to inquire into the State of Defence of the Forts Montgomery and Conſtitution; continued with the Convention and the Committee of Safety at Fiſhkill and Kingſton until 3d April, 1777, when he was directed to

W

repair to the Congrefs at Philadelphia. He remained in Congrefs till December. During the Year 1778 he was detained at Home by Sicknefs. In 1779 he was engaged in collecting Evidence for New York in the Vermont Cafe. He was in Congrefs during a Part of the Years 1780, 1781 and 1782. On the Evacuation of New York he returned to that City, and found his Property very much dilapidated. He was appointed a Member of the Council for the Government of the Southern Diftrict of New York; alfo a Warden of Trinity Church (of which he had been a Veftryman before the Revolution), in which Office he continued during his Refidence in the City. In December, 1783, he was elected State Senator, and on the 5th February, 1784, firft Mayor of the City of New York. In 1788 he was a Member of the Convention which adopted the Conftitution of the United States, and in the following Year was nominated by Wafhington and appointed Diftrict Judge of the Diftrict of New York. This Office he refigned on the 8th April, 1794, and retired from Publick Life. He fettled temporarily in Schenectady, and erected a Church and began building a Houfe for himfelf in Duanefburgh, but did not live to complete it. He died fuddenly 1ft Feb. 1797, aged 64, and was buried under the Church he had erected in Duanefburgh. *(N. Y. Doc. Hift.*, iv, 643-44; *Sargent's Loyalift Poetry*, 157.)

Page 37.

WILLIAM DUER

Was a Son of John Duer, one of the King's Council for the Ifland of Antigua, and was born in England, 18th March, 1747. In his 18th Year he entered the Britifh Service as Aid-de-Camp to Lord Clive, Governor General of India. On the Death of his Father, who left him a handfome pecuniary Legacy, befides an Eftate in Dominica, he left the Army and repaired to the Weft Indies. In 1768 he vifited New York for the Purpofe of procuring Lumber for feveral Plantations, and to avail himfelf of a Contract to furnifh the Britifh Navy with Mafts and Spars. He there became acquainted with Lord Stirling and Philip Schuyler, and by the Recommendation of the latter, purchafed a Tract of Land, including the Falls of Fort Miller, in Wafhington County, N. Y., where he erected Saw Mills, a Grift Mill, a Snuff Mill, and ultimately a Powder Mill. And as he had refolved to make the Place his permanent Refidence, he built a fpacious and commodious Manfion. He had not long refided there, when he was appointed Colonel of the Militia, and a Judge of the County Court, Offices which he held until the Revolution. He was elected a Member of the Provincial Congrefs, and of the Provincial Convention, and was a Member of the Committee of Publick Safety. When the State Conſtitution went into Operation, Col. Duer was elected to the Senate, but before taking his Seat in that Body, was choſen by the Legiſlature a Delegate to the Continental Congreſs. On the 27th July, 1779, he married Catharine, the eldeſt Daughter of Lord Stirling. On the Appointment of Lord Stirling as Commiſſary-General of the Northern Department, Col. Duer removed to Albany, where he remained until the Troops were withdrawn from the Northern Frontier, when he removed to Fiſhkill, where he remained with his Family until 1783. On the Evacuation of New York by the Britiſh Troops, he removed to that City, and made it his permanent Reſidence. He was appointed Secretary of the Board of Commiſſioners of the Treaſury, which Office he filled until the Board was ſuperſeded by the Treaſury Department. He was elected a Member of the State Legiſlature, in order to promote the Grant of the Impoſt Duties, as yet levied by the State, to Congreſs; and after the Adoption of the Conſtitution, was made Aſſiſtant-Secretary of the Treaſury under Hamilton, in which Office he continued until the Seat of Government was removed to Philadelphia. He aſſiſted in forming a Company for the Manufacture of woolen Cloths; and upon its Incorporation by the Legiſlature of New Jerſey, he was placed at its Head; they erected the firſt Mill at the Falls of the Paſſaic, whence has ariſen the flouriſhing Town of Paterſon. At a later Period he eſtabliſhed a Cotton Mill on the Bronx, in the County of Weſtcheſter, which is believed to have been the firſt in this Country. He alſo engaged in Contracts with the Government for furniſhing the Weſtern Army under Gen. Sinclair, during the firſt Indian War, with Clothing, Proviſions and Military Stores. He alſo entered largely into Speculations in Publick Securities, and purchaſed extenſively in the Military Tracts. But his Affairs reached a financial Criſis which proved fatal to his Fortune; his Property was ſacrificed, and he remained for ſome Time without Reſources for the Support of his Family. He died 7th May, 1799, aged 52. (*Knickerbocker Magazine*, XL, 95-103.)

Page 137.

During the Winter of 1777, General Samuel H. Parſons, ſuffering under feeble Health, and a Conſtitution broken down in the Service of his Country, expreſſed to the Commander-in-Chief a Deſire to retire temporarily from the active Duties of the Army, but in Conſequence of the urgent Solicitation of Gen. Waſhington, he relinquiſhed the Deſire, as may appear by the following Letter, dated

"HIGHLANDS, on Hudſon River, 18th Feb'y, 1778.

Dear General: I had the Honor of receiving yours of the 16th of January about eight Days ſince at this Place, where I have returned to take Charge of my Brigade. In the preſent State of the Army, I ſhall continue in my Command, left a different Conduct may prove injurious to the Cauſe of my Country, at this Conjuncture of Affairs. However my Inclination may induce me to retire to the Enjoyment of domeſtic Happineſs, I cannot think myſelf warranted to indulge my Wiſhes at a Time while ſo many Officers under my Command are deſirous of leaving the Toils of War for the Pleaſures of private Life."

About this Time General Putnam went to Connecticut and left *Weſt Point*, and all the Troops ſtationed at the *Highlands*, under the Command of General Parſons, to whom was delegated the additional Duty of *conſtructing Military Works at Weſt Point, which had been delayed in Conſequence of Miſapprehenſion in Regard to the ſeveral Reſolves of Congreſs upon the Subject.* It ſeems that on the 5th of November, 1777, Congreſs appointed General Gates to command in the Highlands, connecting that Poſt with the Northern Department, and empowered him to make Obſtructions in and Fortifications on the Banks of the Hudſon River, but as he was made Preſident of the Board of War, he never entered upon theſe Duties.

Again, on the 18th of February, Gov. Clinton was requeſted to take the Superintendence of the Works, but the Multiplicity of his Civil Employments made it neceſſary for him to decline the Undertaking. Meantime, General Putnam went to Connecticut, and left the Poſt in Charge of Gen. Parſons, who entered promptly upon the diſcharge of his arduous and perplexing Duty.

In a Letter of 18th of February, to General Waſhington, he remarks: "Almoſt every Obſtacle within the Circle of Poſſibility has happened, to retard the Progreſs of the *Obſtructions in and Fortifications on the Banks of Hudſon River.* Preparations for completing them are now in a State which will afford a good Proſpect of completing them in April, and unleſs ſome Difficulties yet unforeſeen ſhould prevent, I think we cannot fail, by the Forepart of that Month to have them in a good Degree of Forwardneſs. Nothing on my Part ſhall be wanting to put them in a State of Forwardneſs to anſwer the reaſonable Expectations of the Country, as early as poſſible."

Again, in a Letter to Gen. Waſhington, dated Camp Weſt Point, 7th of March, 1778, explaining the Perplexities ariſing under the Reſolves of Congreſs of the 5th of November, and 18th February, in regard to Gen.

Gates and Gov. Clinton, whofe Powers were deemed ftrictly *Perfonal,* he remarks :

"In Gen. Putnam's Abfence the Command of the Troops devolves on me with all the Perplexities it is capable of being involved in. I find the Refolve of Congrefs of the 5th of Nov.ʳ directing *the making Obſtruc- tions in and Fortifications on the Banks of Hudſon's River* and empower- ing General Gates to tranfact that Matter are perfonal to Gen. Gates, and give no Order or Authority to the Commanding Officer as fuch. By a Letter from your Excellency to Gen. Putnam of the 2ⁿᵈ Dec.ʳ I find him directed to remove all the Troops from Out Pofts or Commands and attend to fortifying on the River ; another of the 27th of December directs that fmall Parties patrole toward the Plains; by a Refolve of the 18th Feb.ʸ Congrefs empower Gov.ʳ Clinton to fuperintend the Works and to call the Militia of New York, Connecticut, &c. for effecting the Purpofes, and the *Commanding Officer at Peekſkill* is ordered and directed to give him every Affiftance in his Power in forwarding and perfecting the Bufi- nefs committed to him. Governor Clinton *does not chooſe to accept the Appointment,* but in this and every other Matter which will conduce to the Intereft of the Country is willing to afford his Aid and Advice. From this State of Facts your Excellency will fee the difficult and dif- agreeable Situation I am plunged into. The Country expect the Works to be completed as early in the Seafon as poffible. The Powers given by Congrefs are *perfonal* only, and evidently defigned to be fo, and by the Refolves the Commanding Officer has no Authority to concern himfelf about it. Under thefe Circumftances I muft entreat your Excellency's Direction what I fhall do. I moft ardently wifh to aid Gov. Clinton or any other Gentleman appointed to fuperintend the Work; at prefent no Perfon has the Direction, I fuppofe it to be becaufe no Man choofes to be refponfible for the Poft; *I have kept the Troops at Work becauſe I found them here when I took the Command,* and had not particularly at- tended to the Refolves of Congrefs concerning them; I have given Orders and Directions, and caufed Contracts to be made for completing the Works which I now find I had no right to concern myfelf about. Gov- ernor Clinton does not choofe to give any Order about the Matter, left he fhould be thought to accept his Appointment, and although I am con- fcious no Refponce has been incurred by my Orders, but what was ne- ceffary, and the Works are carrying on by the Troops under my Com- mand, yet as I now find I have no Authority for the Purpofe, I do not think I have fufficient Power to juftify me in giving further Orders whereby the Publick may incur an Expence, without fome exprefs Direction for it; Indeed by continuing to do it, I put myfelf in the Power of any Man who may choose to sacrifice me; I am fully of your Excellency's Opinion that the Troops cannot be so well employed in any other way as in perfecting the Obstructions in and Defences near the River and shall continue them here until there is Time to receive your Excellency's further Orders.

By your Excellency's Letter of the 2ᵘᵈ of December, all the Troops are ordered here; by the 27th, Part only are to be employed. By the Resolve of the 5th of November, as many as Gen. Gates shall choose to employ; by that of the 18th Feby none but Militia. Whether your Excellency intends all the Troops to be employed in the Works or part only. Whether the Commanding Officer here shall superintend the Works and hath discretionary Powers to order and direct what he thinks necessary without any Resolve of Congress for the Purpose, where no Person is particularly appointed for the Purpose, or when the Person so appointed refuses to accept, are Questions which very much concern me at present, and which I beg your Excellency to direct me in. The Weather has been such since the 15th of Feby as has greatly retarded us in the Works. About seven Days of the Time has been such that we could do nothing. *I shall exert myself to have them in a State of Defence as early as possible,* so far as I can without any Power whatever, or by the due exercise of such Directions as your Excellency shall please to give me. Col. Radiere finding it impossible to complete the Fort & other Defences intended at this Post in such Manner as to effectually withstand the Attempts of the Enemy to pass up the River early in the Spring, and, not choosing to hazard his Reputation on Works erected on a different Scale, calculated for a short Duration only, has desired leave to wait on your Excellency & Congress, which I have granted him. In Justice to Col. Radiere, I ought to say he appears to be a Gentleman of Science and Knowledge in his Profession, and disposed to render every Service he is able to do. I shall with the Advice of Gov. Clinton expedite the Building such Works as are most necessary for immediate Defence."

To the preceding Letter General Washington replies as follows:

HEADQUARTERS, Valley Forge, }
5th March, 1778. }

"Dear Sir: I am favored with yours of the 18th Feby. I am exceedingly glad to hear your Determination to remain in the Army at this Time, when too many are withdrawing themselves from the Service, and I am not less pleased at the Account you give me of the *Progress of the Obstructions and Fortifications in and upon the River.* I can only recommend your strictest Attention to a Work of so much Consequence. I must also desire that you will have all the Arms at the different Posts in your Neighborhood collected, and have thofe that want Repair put into the Hands of the Armourers at Fifhkill, for I am certain when we come to draw our Force together in the Spring, that we fhall want Arms, notwithftanding the confiderable Importations. Col. Hay of Haverftraw informs me, that there is a large Quantity of Forage collected at that Place, which he fears will fall into the Enemy's Hands if it is not removed or a proper Guard fent over to protect it. As your Force will not probably allow you to do the latter with Convenience, I wifh you would do all in your Power to effect the former. The Enemy, I fhould fuppofe, muft be diftreffed for want of it, and when our Stores come forward in the Spring our Horfes will ftand in need of it. As Col. Hay complains of Gen¹ Putnam's Inattention to this Matter when he reprefented it to him, I muft beg you to fee to it.

The Committee of Congrefs who are now here have defired that no Commiffions be filled up till fome new general Arrangements of the Army are completed. The Gentlemen will not loofe any of their Pretenfions to Rank, by waiting a little Time longer for their Commiffions, which fhall be forwarded as foon as the Bufinefs above mentioned is finifhed.

Col. Webb's Officers will take Rank from the Time he really appointed them. As I do not know when that was, he or Lieut. Col. Livingfton muft make an exact Return of their Ranks and Time of Appointment, &c.

I am Dear Sir,

Yours, &c.

G. Washington.

Again, in another Letter General Wafhington addreffed General Parfons (then at New York), as follows:

Head Quarters, Valley Forge,
7 March, 1778.

"Dear Sir: In a Letter from General Putnam of the 13th ult° he informed me, that there were two large Scows and feveral Gunboats upon Hand, and that the Timber for two floating Batteries was cut, but the Work not begun; I muft beg your Attention to the completing of thefe feveral Kinds of Craft and to the repairing of any others that may want it. We fhall have occafion for the common Boats to tranfport Men, Baggage and Stores with Expedition, when we are drawing our Reinforcements from the Eaftward, and for the armed Boats and Batteries to keep open the Communication, fhould any of the Enemy's Veffels attempt to interrupt it. Gen. Putnam wrote me at the fame Time that fome Boats were building at Albany, but did not know in what Forwardnefs they were. Be pleafed to inform yourfelf and urge the Neceffity of having them finifhed."

To the two preceding Letters General Parſons replied as follows:

"CAMP WEST POINT, March 16, 1778.

"Dear General: On the 14th inſt. I had the Honor of receiving your Letter of the 7th of March, and alſo one of the 8th containing a Copy of the 5th of March. I ſhall pay particular Attention to forwarding the Work of the Boats deſigned for tranſporting over, as well as thoſe which are to be employed for Defenſe on Hudſon River. I have ordered all the Boats and other Crafts on the River to be collected in different Places and put to the beſt poſſible State immediately. I have not got a Return, when that is made I ſhall be able to give your Excellency a particular Account of them. When I was laſt at Poughkeepſie the Gun Boats were in ſuch a State as to give Hopes of their being fit for Uſe within a few Weeks, and as Gov. Clinton has been kind enough to take upon himſelf the Direction of them, I think we may hope to ſee them completed ſoon. I will ſend to Albany and know the State of the Boats there, and as the River will ſoon be clear of Ice, I will order down ſuch Boats and other Crafts as can be had there, fit for Tranſportation over the River. *If the Chain is completed we ſhall be ready to ſtretch it over the River next Week.* A ſufficient Number of Chevaux de friſe to fill thoſe Parts left open laſt Year, are ready to ſink as ſoon as the Weather and the State of the River will admit it to be done. I hope to have *two Sides and one Baſtion of the Fort* in ſome State of Defence in about a Fortnight, the other Sides need very little to ſecure them. There is a Proſpect of having five or ſix Cannon mounted in one of our Batteries this Week. I think the Works are going on as faſt as could be expected from our ſmall Number of Men, total Want of Materials provided, and of Money to purchaſe them. We have borrowed, and begged, and hired Money to this Time. I have ſeveral times advanced my laſt Shilling towards purchaſing Materials, &c., and I believe this has been the Caſe with almoſt every Officer here. As we ſtill live, I hope we ſhall accompliſh the Works in the River in Seaſon, if the Enemy move with their accuſtomed Caution and Tardineſs; when I hope Congreſs will repay what has been advanced, and cannot think us blamable if we have been compelled to ſubject the Country to ſome extra Expence to ſave the Public Credit and forward the Buſineſs intruſted to our Care. By a Letter from General Putnam, I ſhall expect his Return to this Poſt by the End of this Week. He has purchaſed three 18 Pounders mounted on travelling Carriages, which are on the Road from Boſton. The Contents of your Excellency's Letter of the 8th ſhall be particularly attended to, if no other Difficulties appear than at preſent offer themſelves to View, perhaps an Attempt may be made within eight Days, much ſooner it cannot be for Reaſons I will hereafter give. The Letter of the 5th refer'd to in that of the 8th, not having come to Hand, gives me fome Concern, as that falling into the Enemy's Hands may wholly defeat us; I fhall be unwilling to make the Attempt unlefs it fhould arrive fafe. The Horfe mentioned by your Excellency cannot be had, one Horfeman only being at this Poft at prefent, but fome other Mode may be fubftituted.

I am your Excellency's

Obe^t Servt,

Sam H. Parsons

Again, in Reference to the Movements of the Enemy at New York, &c., General Parfons thus writes to General Wafhington, under Date,

Fishkill, 20 March, 1778.

" Dear General : By a Variety of Accounts from New York, the Enemy defign'd fpeedy Movement from thence; about thirty Tranfports are in Ballaft, Cannon taken on board and Troops marched from Kings Bridge to the City laft Sunday. Where their Deftination is I cannot conjecture from the Information I have rec^d. I hope not up this River until our Defence is more perfect. I this Moment hear the Fleet failed the Day before yefterday, and are faid to be bound Eaftward. They went toward the Hook from New York. Your Excellency's Letter of the 5th I received the 18th Inftant & fhall purfue your Directions.

I am your Excellency's

Obe^t Servt,

Sam'l H. Parsons.

Letter from General McDougall to General Parfons.

Head Quarters, Fifhkill, 4th April, 1778.

Sir :

I received yours of 25 m. paft 8 o'Clock of this Morning. Thofe Veffels are probably coming up to reconnoitre the State of your Works, whatever may be their Object. The completing the Works and Ob-

X

ftruΔions are of fo much Importance, that you muft defend the Ground to the utmoft of your Power, for fhould the Enemy deftroy thofe Works and Barracks, the compleating the Works and ObftruΔions cannot be accomplifhed this Campaign. If the Enemy fhould appear in tolerable Force, your Strength fhould be difpofed in the beft Pofition to defend Weft Point. I fhall be obliged to rifque the . . . . here to the Defence of the Militia, till the Continental Troops arrive from below and Albany; you did right to order the Stores from Kings Ferry. Mr. Mudock has fent off a Number of Stores to you this Morning; if the 18 Pound Cartridges are not fent, I have ordered my Aid to him to difpatch them with the Whaleboat and 24 Rounds of Mufket Cartridges for 700 Men. A Mortar will be of little ufe to you againft a Ship; as her Movement, even when fhe is at anchor, is fo various with Wind and Tide. The Howitzer which you have will be of more ufe to you. A good Lookout as far down the River as your Boats can go with Safety; and the inclofing the Work fhould be fteadily purfued. If their three Veffels fhould come near, your Scouts fhould be fent out on both Sides of the River, where it is probable they may land a fmall Party to reconnoitre the State of your Works. Thefe are the general ObjeΔs I wifh you to attend to. I have this Morning wrote for Colonel Nixon's Regiment, and fuggefted to Governor Clinton the Neçeffity of having the Militia in a State of Readinefs. If the Enemy vifit you foon, I fhall do every thing in my Power for your Relief; you have now all the Force I can give you; unlefs I call the Militia out. And if this is done, upon the appearance of three Veffels, they will not turn out fo readily, when they may be wanted for ferious Service. Captain Sloo with his Men, and Boats are fo expofed to be cut off, by a fmall Party from thofe Veffels, or any other, that I wifh you to order him to fend up all the Boats and Scows except two, and their Crews to Fifhkill Landing, and in Cafe he finds himfelf in Danger to remove there to Ply,[1] as I have no Guard to give him. The Returns of the Corps at Weft Point, will be made every Friday, and the Command particularly defignated at the Return. If you can fend to him by Water, caufe the inclofed to be delivered to Major Thearfe.

I am in Hafte,

Your Humble Servant,

ALEX. McDOUGALL.

General Parfons.

---

[1] *Query*, to remove thence to the Fly, (or *Vlaie*.)

Letter from General Parfons to Col. Jeremiah Wadfworth.

CAMP AT WEST POINT, Feb. 22, 1778.

DEAR SIR :

Your Favor of the 9th inft. I rec'd by Col. Hughes, and thank you for the Care you have taken of me. You afk me where I can be found ? This is a puzzling Queftion ; the Camp is at a Place on Hudfon's River cal'd Weft Point, oppofite where Fort Conftitution once ftood. The fituation is pas'd Defcription, furrounded with almoft inacceffible Mountains, and craggy Rocks which overtop the higheft Hills, at prefent covered with Piles of Snow, the River in our Front affords a beautiful Profpeft on our Right and Left to New Windfor on one Hand and to Fort Montgomery on ye other with fome little Iflands interfpers'd. The furrounding Profpeft affords as great Variety of Hills, Mountains, Rocks, which feem to fhut up every Avenue to us, and of Swamps, Meadows, deep Vallies which obftruft the Paffage of the Traveller and of fmall beautiful Plains in a good Degree of Cultivation intermixed, as almoft any Place I have feen ; to a contemplative Mind which delights in a lonely Retreat from the World to view and admire the ftupendous and magnificent Works of Nature, 'tis as beautiful as Sharon, but affords to a Man who loves the Society of the World a profpeft nearly allied to the Shades of Death ; here I am to be found at prefent in what Situation of Mind you will eafily imagine. Mr. Dwight and Major Humphrey are now here, and a good Companion now and then adds to the Number of my agreeable Family.

News arrives here by Accident only. The account of Burgoine's Defeat reach'd the Ears of Adminiftration via Carleton about the 5th of Dec. (I dare fay 'twas fent by him with Expedition and good Relifh). The Nation was put into a great Confternation, but after three or four Days recovered their furprife and voted 20,000 additional Troops about the 8th of Dec'r.

I am heartily glad Col. Delancy has returned, the more fo, as the Gentry of this State were flufh'd with Hopes he would violate his Honour and aft the bafe Part they wifh'd, tho at prefent he cannot be exchang'd, nothing on my Part fhall be omitted to render the State of a Prifoner as eafy to him as a Man of Honor has Reafon to expeft ; my Compliments await him, with my Wifhes that his *perfonal* Enemies may never have greater caufe to Triumph over him than his prefent Conduft has afforded. Col. Webb, I hear, will not be exchang'd at prefent, perhaps 'tis Right. I earneftly wifh to know what we are about in Connefticut, what profpefts of filling and fupporting our Army, &c. * * * *

General Parsons to Governor Trumbull.

[Trumbull's Papers, vol. VIII, p. 92. Mass. Hist. Soc'y.]

FISHKILL, 27th Feb., 1778.

SIR :

The Diſtreſs of the Southern Army is doubtleſs made known to your Excellency. No mode of Relief will be left untried to relieve them, the Proviſions on the Border of your State and of New York cannot be remov'd without the Aid of Teams, and the Army muſt periſh without them ; and the Teams cannot be furniſh'd in this State, 'tis too late to Speculate about the Matter; without the immediate coercive Power of your Government, in my Opinion, the Army is ruin'd ; I muſt therefore earneſtly entreat your Excellency to iſſue Orders to impreſs neceſſary Teams for the purpoſe of removing Proviſions, &c., to the North River, and that the Order made may be tranſmitted to this Poſt without Delay, that I may be enabled to know what Meaſures to take in purſuance thereof.

General Waſhington to General Parſons, at Weſt Point.

[P—vol. I, No. 32, p. 64.]

VALLEY FORGE, March 8th, 1778.

DEAR SIR :

Below you will receive a Copy of my laſt, dated the 5th, to which I will add a Thought which has occurred ſince the writing of it ; and which, if the Scheme is praĉticable at all, may add not a little to the Succeſs; namely, to let the Officers and Soldiers employed in the Enterpriſe be dreſſed in red, and much in the Taſte of the Britiſh Soldiery. Webb's Regiment will afford theſe Dreſſes ; and it might not be amiſs to know certainly, the Number of ſome Regiment that is quartered in the City. Under ſome Circumſtances this Knowledge may avail them, eſpecially of the Number on their own Buttons ſhould correſpond thereto.

P. S. The Official Papers would be a vaſt Acquiſition, and might without much Difficulty, accompany the Perſon.

Copy of the Letter referred to.

March 5th, 1778.

DEAR SIR:

I learn from undoubted Authority, that General Clinton quarters in Captain Kennedy's Houfe, in the City of New York, which you know is near Fort George, and by the late Fire ftands in a Manner alone. What Guards may be at, or near, his Quarters, I cannot with Precifion fay; and, therefore, fhall not add any thing on this Score, leaft it fhould prove a Mif-information : But I think it one of the moft practicable (and furely it will be amongft the moft defirable and honourable) Things imaginable, to take him Prifoner.

This Houfe laying clofe on the Water, and a retired Way through a back Yard or Garden leading into it, what, if you have Whale Boats (8 or 10) but want of Secrecy, can prevent the Execution in the Hands of an enterprifing Party. The Embarkation might even be (and this I fhould think beft) at King's Ferry, on the firft of the Ebb, and early in the Evening. Six or eight Hours, with change of Hands, would row the Boats under the Weft Shore, and very fecretly to the City, and the flood Tide will hoift them back again; or a Party of Horfe might meet them at Fort Lee.

I had like not to have mentioned that no Ship of War is in the North River (was not at leaft) ten Days ago, nor within 400 Yards of the Point; all being in the Eaft River. I fhall add no more. This is dropped as a Hint, to be improved upon, or rejected, as Circumftances point out and juftify.

[From the Connecticut Gazette, No. 750, March 27, 1778.]

CAMP WEST POINT, March 8, 1778.

All the Officers not on the recruiting Service, and Soldiers belonging to the feveral Regiments in the Brigade under my Command, who have been abfent on Furloughs which are now expired, are to join their re-fpective Regiments without Lofs of Time. This Order is to be confid-ered as the moft peremptory, and no Excufe but Inability will be admitted for want of Compliance.

And whereas there are many Deferters from General Howe's Army and from the Troops lately commanded by General Burgoyne, fome Prifoners of War, who have been fuffered to remain at large, and divers fuſpicious or difaffected Perſons ſtrolling about the Country, who are daily offering themſelves for Enliſtments.

The ſeveral commiſſioned and non-commiſſioned Officers now on the recruiting Service, are directed and ordered in the moſt poſitive Terms not to enliſt any Perſons of the above Deſcription or give Certificates concerning ſuch Perſons if hired for the Purpoſe of exempting any Inhabitants of theſe States from military Duty.

And the Gentlemen employed by the Legiſlatures of the States, for promoting the recruiting Service are deſired to take Notice of the above Prohibition, and regulate their Conduct accordingly.

SAMUEL H. PARSONS, Brig' General.

Gen. Parſons to Capt. Thomas Machin, at New Windſor.

WEST POINT, 11th March, 1778.

SIR:

As Col. Labradier has left us, I wiſh you, if you can be abſent from New Windſor for a Day, to come to this Poſt tomorrow or the Day after, to adviſe about the proper Method of fortifying this Place.

General Waſhington to General Parſons, at Weſt Point.

[B—vol. v, No. 172, p. 153.]

HEAD QUARTERS, 18th March, 1778.

DEAR SIR:

I am favoured with yours of the 7th, encloſing a Letter from the Rev'd Mr. Dwight, to whom I have written upon the Matter propoſed by him.

I am ſorry to hear, that any ſeeming Inconfiſtency in my Letters ſhould, among other Things, have retarded the Execution of the Works, but if you will revert to my Letters of the 2d and 27th of December, you will find that my Orders were expreſs, to keep the Troops, meaning the main Body of them, ſteadily to work. I mentioned a Liberty of ſending out light Parties towards the Plains, becauſe they were neceſſary, not only to curb ſmall foraging Parties of the Enemy, but for the Security of the Camp.

To reconcile all Matters, and to obviate the Jealouſies and Prejudices that, whether well or ill-founded, had taken Place, I have ordered General McDougall to take the Command at the Highlands, and veſted him

Appendix.   183

with full Powers to fuperintend the whole, at leaft, until Congrefs have determined whether the Command of the Forts and the Superintendency of the Works fhall be diftinct and independent of that Department.

General Wafhington to Maj. Gen. McDougall, at Fifhkill.

[Wafhington's Writings, B—vol. v, p. 200, No. 220.]

[Extract.]   VALLEY FORGE, March 31ft, 1778.

By Report, Rhode Ifland was to be evacuated (as on the 20th inft.) and the Opinion brought to Philadelphia. This, if true, evidently proves that Gen. Howe intends an early Campaign, to take Advantage of our weak State. What is to be done? We muft either oppofe our whole Force to his, in this Quarter, or take the Advantage of him in fome other, *which leads me to afk your Opinion of the Practicability of an Attempt upon New York with Parfon's Brigade, Nixon's, and the Regiments of Van Schaick,* Hazen and James Livingfton's, *aided by the Militia from the States of New York and Connecticut,* fuch I mean as can fpeedily be drawn together. *On this Subject and the advifability of fuch* an Enterprife, I would have you confult *Gov. Clinton and Gen. Parfons, and them only.*

General Alexander McDougall to General Wafhington.

[Wafhington's Papers, vol. xxii, p. 182.]

[Extract.]   FISHKILL, 13th April, 1778.

SIR:

I am honored with the Receipt of your Favor of the 31ft ult° and 6th inft. The Inclofures in the laft have been forwarded agreeable to your Orders.

No Service would be more agreeable to me than an Attack upon New York could recommend it confiftent with any probable Profpect of Succefs. But the Condition and Strength of thefe Pofts utterly forbid it; efpecially when the Confequence of a Misfortune in the Attempt is duly confidered, as it may affect the Supplies to your Army and the general Influence of the Campaign.

When I have more Leifure I fhall enumerate the Reafons on which I give *this Opinion.*

For the prefent I beg leave to refer your Excellency to *that* of *Gov-*

ernor Clinton and *General Parfons,*[1] &c. Mr. Kofciufko is efteemed by thofe who have attended the Works at Weft Point, to have more Practice than Col. Delaradiere, and his Manner of treating the People more acceptable than that of the latter; which induced *General Parfons* and Governor Clinton to defire the former may be continued at Weft Point. The firft has a Commiffion as Engineer with the Rank of Colonel in October, 1776; Col. Delaradiere's Commiffion I think is dated in November laft.

General Parfons to General McDougall, on State of Provifions in his Department.

[General Gates's Papers, vol. xii, in N. Y. Hift. Society.]

LYME, 27 April, 1778.

DEAR GENERAL:

I have carefully examined the State of Provifions in the Commiffary Department, and believe the Meat in this State already purchafed will fupply the Army to about the 10th June, from which there will be fome Diftrefs in the Army for that Article for fome fhort Time, perhaps to the Middle of July, unlefs fupplied from other States, fouthward and weftward of this. Governor Trumbull is very defirous to purfue the propofed Attack on New York, and will do what any Man can do to forward the Defign. He defires the Troops may not be called for until our Preparations are made, that they may be detained as little Time as poffible; but in the Interim he would wifh to be informed early whether the Defign is purfued or laid afide. The important Advice from France and

---

1 Vol. 23, p. 22 "That the Regiment propofed be fent forward, that Preparations be immediately made, with as much Difpatch as poffible to execute the Whole or fuch Part of the propofed Plan, as Circumftances will admit of; that Application be made to Gov. Trumbull, to know what Number of the new made Regiments can be had, and at what Time; that the Commiffary-General be alfo applied to, for an Account o f Provifions, &c. That the Enterprize does not promife Succefs by Coup de main, under prefent Circumftances; but there may be great Probability of its fucceeding in the whole or in part, within a Month, or five Weeks, if Men and Provifions can be made. The prefent State of the Pofts, for the Defence of the North River, does not admit withdrawing the Troops for the propofed Expedition immediately, but in a few Weeks the Works may be in fome State of Defence, fo as to be tenable with fewer Men, than at prefent and the Confequences lefs fatal to the Country in Cafe of the Expedition's failing in the Execution.

SAM'L H. PARSONS,
GEO. CLINTON.

the evident Diſtreſs of Britain, in my Opinion, affords us the beſt Opportunity of attacking the Enemy with the faireſt Proſpeĉts of Succeſs; long
Delays I fear will be detrimental, eſpecially when the inſidious Arts of
the Britiſh Court have begun to be praĉticed & may have too baneful an
Influence if they are ſuffered to continue long in their preſent State. I
wiſh to hear from your Honor by the Return of Poſt; that if my continuance in this State, any longer, can be of any public Utility, I may receive your Orders; otherwiſe I believe I ſhall be able to return in about a
Fortnight. If we make the propoſed Attack, I am of Opinion I ſhall be
of more Service by ſtaying here till the Order is made & the Levies
nearly completed which are expeĉted from this State, than I can be at
your Poſt.

General Parſons to General Horatio Gates.

[Gates Papers, New York Hiſtorical Society.]

WEST POINT, 31 May, 1778.

DEAR GENERAL:

Major Humphrey has juſt returned, and reports that the 52d Reg't
commanded by Col. French, marched from New York the 23d inſt.,
and encamped near Kings Bridge in a Line with the 45th. The 71ſt
Reg't have arrived at the Bridge from Long Iſland; the Regiments of the
Hereditary Prince, Prince Charles, of Trumback, of Stein, are all the
Foreign Troops he could learn remained on York Iſland; two of which
are in the Bowery near the City, and two near Kings Bridge; the 38th
Britiſh Reg't is in the City; moſt, if not all, the new Levies are marched
from the Bridge to the City, about 8 Days ſince, Part of them embarked
on Board Ships at Horn's Hook; the Public Report is they are going to
Long Iſland to replace the Troops which have been called from thence
to the Bridge. 'Tis publickly reported that a French War aĉtually
exiſts at this Time; the Preſs was very hot in New York; the Accounts
of the Numbers obtained in this way are various from 250 to 1000,
however they all agree they are for the Sea Service and are put on Ship
board. A conſiderable number of Shipping were in the Eaſt River a
few Days ſince, and the Evening of the 29th a Fleet from New York
came to anchor in the Sound near Hart Iſland oppoſite Eaſt Cheſter and
New Rochelle, ſuppoſed to be about 20 or 30 Ships; a Preſs is expeĉted
every Day upon Long Iſland; the Refugees are concealing themſelves to
avoid it.

All Communication with the City has been prohibited for ſome

Y

Time, evidently to cover their Movements, this being effected, the Inhabitants are again permitted to pafs over the Bridge with Provifions, &c. On the whole 'tis pretty evident inftead of collecting a Force at the Bridge, their Strength is leffened, and the new Levies have doubtlefs bufinefs in fome other Quarter; a Paper of the 25th of May, from New York, I have fent you. When I have the honor to wait on you I fhall be able to give fome more particular Accounts.

I underftand you defign to vifit the Troops at Peekfkill to-Day, and I fhall therefore call upon you in the Morning.

General Parfons to General Gates.

[Gates Papers, New York Hiftorical Society.]

WEST POINT, 4th June, 1778.

DEAR GENERAL:

The Artilleriſts at the Point are by no means fufficient in Number to manage the Artillery here. Col. Stevens' three Companies may be very ufefully employed at this Poft. Their Numbers will enable us to put the Artillery in a proper State. If no fpecial purpofe is to be anfwered by removing them to this Village, I fhall be much obliged by Colonel Stevens and his Men remaining at this Poft for the prefent. If any Companies of the Train are wanted at the Village more than are now there a Company of Col. Lamb's Regiment, perhaps on many accounts, had better be fent; that Regiment has been in contention from their raifing, and I am certain Captain Moody and Colonel Stevens will never agree in the fame Camp. As foon as the weather will permit 'twill be neceffary for them to encamp; if your Honor fhall be of opinion the Service will be as well advanced by their continuing here as removing, I fhould be happy in his receiving your Order to take his Poft at this Place.

Will it be neceffary to publifh in General Orders that Colonel Stevens commands the Artillery? Many unhappy difputes may be prevented by it.

General Parfons to General Gates.

[Gates Papers, New York Hiftorical Society.]

WEST POINT, 8th June, 1778.

DEAR GENERAL :

By the information of Deferters and the concurring Accounts of Inhabitants near the Bridge, there are 3 Heffian and 2 Britifh Regiments in the City, 1 Battallion of Highlanders at Blomingdale ; at Ft. Wafhington and the Bridge, 2 Britifh Regiments, viz : the 45th and 52d, two Heffian Regiments, Bruverton's and Bayard's Regiments and Emmerick's Chaffeurs, 1 twelve and 6 fix Pounders in Fort Independence ; 2 of 18, 2 of 12 and 5 of 6 and under in Fort Wafhington. The Cannon removed from the Embrafures in Fort Wafhington on the Side next the North River. Fort Independence not picketted but an Abattis around it ; a Captain's Guard kept in the Fort relieved every three Days ; in the Redoubts are Guards from 25 to 36 Men, By the Information of returning Refugees, it appears the Enemy are eftablifhing a Camp at the Head of the Fly on Long Ifland. Cruger's, Ludlow's, Fanning's and a Reg't of Brown's Brigade, are to encamp there, perhaps 1000 Men. A Reg't of Regular Tories at Brookline, I fuppofe the 35th, this Reg't rec'd orders laft Tuefday to march Eaftward on the Ifland, and their heavy Baggage to be put on Ship Board, by the Information of Jos. Lawrence and Samuel Riker, from New York, two Britifh Regiments received Orders to embark the 6th inft., but where deftined is uncertain. No particular information of Robinfon's Regiment. I think it probable they ftill remain at Harlem. The Ships are thirty man'd and cannot remove without increafing the Number of Hands. Thofe at Huntington are ordered to be ready to fail fome Time next Week. The Enemy are ftrengthening their Works on Bayard's Hill, but in what Manner I am unable to learn ; On the whole Matter it appears evident to me, the Enemy are not preparing to make any capital Attack on the Country, but are fecuring themfelves from any Attempt we may make in the City.

The Camp at the Fly on Long Ifland, I think well chofen to defend the City on that Part. 'Tis about eight or nine Miles from the Ferry, and from the Creek near the Camp to Jamaica Bay on the South of the Ifland about five miles ; and the Paffes through the Mountains are effectually fecured by this Poft which leaves it exceeding difficult to move forward to Brookline with any Artillery ; and will enable the Enemy to fend occafional Parties down the Ifland and compel what Supplies of Provifions and Forage from Suffolk County can be fpared. I believe that County can feed three thoufand Men fix Months.

W. Malcom to General Parfons.

WEST POINT, Auguft 3, 1778.

DEAR GENERAL:

Here I am holding Committee among Spades and Shovels. Why was I banifhed? However I begin to be reconciled. I muft be fo; efpecially as you are not moving towards York; if you do don't be furprifed to fee me parade among you. We are driving on downwards; the more we do the more we find we have to do. Why did you not begin to move the Mountain, rather than add to its Magnitude. Send me News and Newfpapers, anything to keep us alive, this is actually t'other End of the World. My Compliments to his Grace and my other good Friends and Acquaintances in your Family. I often think with pleafure on the Happinefs of the few paft Weeks we were together, but it adds to my Vexation too.

General Parfons's Opinion in Anfwer to Queries of his Excellency Gen'l Wafhington in his Letters of the 14th and 15th October, 1778.

CAMP, October 17th, 1778.

SIR:

The march of Part of the Troops towards Bofton being determined, it only remains for me to give my Opinion in what Manner the Army fhall be difpofed during the Winter, and how they are to be provided with Forage and Provifions.

The Security, good Government, and Difcipline of the Troops will be beft attained and promoted in a compact Body, and Bread will be eafier fupplied in a Station near the North River than in any other Pofition, and no other Pofition will fo effectually fecure our important Pofts near that River. Forage will be provided with greater Eafe and at lefs Expenfe in a difperfed than a compact Situation. I imagine the greater Part of the Meat confumed in the Winter will be falted, the Grafs fed Beef will foon be expended, and the Stall fed Beef will not be furnifhed in great Quantities until near the Clofe of the Winter; if this fhould be the cafe, the Expenfe of Carriage will be lefs in a difperfed than a united Situation.

On the whole, I am of Opinion, that about 6 or 7000 Men fhould be kept in a collected Body at or near Fifhkill, which with the Affiftance of the Militia, will be able to Defend thofe Paffes againft any Force the Enemy can bring againft them before the whole Army might be again united ; that about 1000 be pofted in the Garrifon at Weft Point, about 3000 at or near the Clove on the weft Side Hudfon's River, and the Remainder (about 2000) not far from Danbury or Ridgefield, or in that proportion, fhould the Army be more or lefs numerous after the firft of January, by which Time the term of Service of many in the Army expires. Thefe Pofts will be fo far removed from the Enemy as to fecure againft any fudden Attack of the Enemy, and will enable them with Safety to fend off moft of their Horfes and Cattle. The Guards for preferving the Paffage by King's Ferry to the Southern from the Eaftern States may be furnifhed from Fifhkill ; and the intermediate Guards neceffary from Danbury and the Clove.

The Poft at Danbury may furnifh Guards on the Sea Coaft, to prevent Incurfions of fmall Parties of the Enemy to defolate their Towns or pillage their Property, and although no Protection can be afforded the Towns on the Sea Coafts fufficient to prevent their Deftruction by a large Detachment of the Enemy ; yet a Protection from the Incurfions of fmall Parties, will be a great relief to the Inhabitants ; and a Body of Troops ftationed near the Coafts may probably prevent the Enemy from making thofe Attempts which otherwife would be made.

But a Reafon which has great Weight in my Mind, is the great Diffatis-faction which will be given the Country, if this Meafure is not purfued. I cannot omit again expreffing to your Excellency my Fears that the prefent Temper of the Country, the difcontent and increafing Uneafinefs of the Army, the depreciated State of our Currency, and other Caufes not neceffary to enumerate, afford the Enemy a fair Opportunity yet to plunge us into inextricable Ruin and Deftruction. If thefe Fears are juftly grounded, great Attention ought to be paid to the Inclinations and Wifhes of the Inhabitants of the States, as one Mode of preventing thofe Confequences which may follow from the prefent State of the Country.

This difpofition is fufficiently numerous in every Part to keep up regular Difcipline, and in cafe of an Attack may foon be fupported ; and will ferve as a Nucleus to which the Militia will gather, and with whom they will be able to make an effectual Oppofition to any Detachment the Enemy can fend.

General Wafhington to General Putnam.

HEAD QUARTERS, MIDDLEBROOK, April 28, '79.

DEAR SIR :

By Intelligence received from different Quarters, there is great Reafon to fufpect the Enemy have fome important Movement in Contemplation. In this Afpect of things it becomes the part of Prudence to provide as effectually as we can for the Security of thofe Points, at which we are moft vulnerable. I am therefore to defire, you will without delay detach *General Parfons's Brigade* to reinforce General McDougall, and to continue with him 'till further Orders. They muft take their Artillery and Baggage with them.

General Wafhington to General Putnam.

MIDDLEBROOK, May 24, 1779.

DEAR SIR :

By recent Intelligence through different Channels I have the beft reafon to believe, that General Clinton has drawn his whole Force to a Point at New York and its Vicinity. That he has collected, and fome accounts add, removed to Kingfbridge, a number of flat bottomed Boats with muffled Oars, and that every Appearance indicates an Expedition at Hand. There are but two important Objects he can have in View, towit : This Army and the Pofts in the Highlands. Should either be attempted therefore, or a Movement made, which has a tendency to either, you will caufe *General Parfons's Brigade*, to march without a moment's lofs of Time for the Highlands, and put them under the Orders of Major General McDougall. Every Preparation is to be made in the Mean while for this Event, that no Delay may happen, after a Call from General McDougall, or your Knowledge of the Matter, previoufly obtained through any other Channel. The Brigade may move by the way of Mahopack Pond, to be equally in the Way to Peekfkill or Fifhkill, fubject neverthelefs, to any other Route, which Circumftances may induce Gen'l McDougall to give. Baggage is to be no impediment to the March, for as the Occafion, more than probably, will be urgent, the March and Junction with the Troops on the North River muft be rapid.

Brig. Gen. Parfons's Opinion of the proper Difpofition of the Army.

WEST POINT, 12th June, 1779.

DEAR GENERAL:

General Paterfon joined his Brigade laft Evening, and is now on the Point; when the Public Service will admit, I fhall be happy to join my Brigade at fuch place as will moft conduce to the general Welfare.

Your Excellency was pleafed to defire my Opinion of the difpofition to be made of the Army.

Under all circumftances, I think 3000 Men fhould be affigned for garrifoning this Poft, by which I underftand the Forts on the Point and Highlands near the Heights near Rock Hill, and the Ifland where Fort Conftitution was.

On the Eaft Side the River, a Force fhould be kept in the Highlands fufficient to prevent the Enemy's occupying the Hills there which may cover Works, which will exceedingly diftrefs this Poft. The advance of thofe Troops may fafely be at or near the Village; this I think neceffary, becaufe thofe Grounds cannot be held by this Garrifon, without new Works are conftructed and the Garrifon increafed. The remainder of the Army will be well pofted in or near Smith's Clove, with a Detachment advanced between Fort Montgomery and the Furnace.

As this Poft, or the Army, are the only capital Objects the Enemy can propofe, I do not know a better Difpofition which can be made at prefent to defeat their Defigns, than what may be formed on the Ideas before expreffed.

I have nothing new this Day, neither my Scouts nor my Boats are yet returned. I fhould be obliged to your Excellency to be informed what Congrefs have Refolved refpecting an Aid-de-Camp for a Brigadier, that I may recommend one if allowed.

Major General Heath to Brigadier Gen. Parfons,

HEAD QUARTERS,
DANFORTH'S HOUSE, June 25, 1779.

DEAR SIR:

I have this moment received a Letter from his Excellency General Wafhington, in which is a Paragraph in the following Words: " I " think it will be advifeable to detach a couple hundred Men towards

" Robinſon's Stores at Mahopach Pond, to march light and with Caution
" endeavoring to magnify their Numbers to the Inhabitants. This may
" ſerve to check the Enemy and help to diſcover their Deſign."

In Conſequence whereof you will pleaſe to detach as ſoon as may be,
one Field Officer, and one hundred Light Infantry properly officered ;
this Detachment from your Brigade will be joined by one hundred from
General Huntington's Brigade. As I do not fully know the beſt Route I
requeſt you would direct one and point out to General Huntington the
Place where the Infantry of the two Brigades ſhall form a Junction, and
at what Hour. My dear Sir, let no Time be loſt. If poſſible let the
Men have a little Rum with them and ſuch Proviſions as may be neceſſary.

*Brig. Gen. Parſons's Opinion in Anſwer to Queries of his
Excellency Gen'l Waſhington in Proceedings of Council
of General Officers of 26th July,* 1779.

CAMP NEAR ROBINSON'S, 27th July, 1779.

DEAR GENERAL :

The ſuppoſed Strength of the Enemy, and our own Numbers and
Preparations, as ſtated by your Excellency to the Council, will in my
Opinion oblige us to adopt a defenſive Syſtem, until our Army is conſi-
derably increaſed in Numbers and other Preparations for offenſive Operations. The Poſts in the Highlands are of ſo much Importance as ought
to induce us to defend them at every Hazard ; for that purpoſe I ſuppoſe
three thouſand Men neceſſary to be left at the Point and Poſts dependant,
if the Army moves to any great Diſtance. Forage for the Cattle and
Horſes will neceſſarily oblige us to remove very ſoon.

I believe, if the Right of the Army ſhould take a Poſition at Peekſkill,
and extend the Left nearly to the Poſt now occupied by Gen'l Glover,
and wait Events, it will in no Meaſure oppoſe a Syſtem of Defence ; they
will be perfectly ſafe from Attack, will be eaſily furniſhed with neceſſary
Supplies, and be in a better Situation to carry on a partiſan War, than
in their preſent Poſition ; and can be ready in Seaſon to relieve the
Fort in caſe of an Attack ; and to oppoſe with Proſpects of Succeſs any
Attempts which may be made to deſtroy the Towns on the Coaſt or
Frontier of Connecticut. If we can procure a Sufficiency of Military
Stores for the Purpoſe, I am of Opinion an Attempt to diſpoſſeſs the
Enemy of Verplanks and Stony Points ought to be attempted ; this, if
ſucceſsful, would diſgrace the Britiſh Arms, animate our Soldiery to

greater Exertions, and enable us to move with Safety to a greater Diſtance from Weſt Point, and thereby cover a larger Extent of Country from the Enemy's Depredations; beſides, they will be removed to ſo great a diſtance from the Point, as to put it out of their Power to make any ſudden Attack upon the Fort; if this Enterpriſe ſhould be undertaken, both Sides of the River ſhould be attempted at the ſame Time, becauſe the Poſt on the Eaſt Side cannot be carried whilſt the Enemy remain poſſeſſed of Stony Point. In this Poſition of the Army the Enemy can advance no Part of their Force to any conſiderable Diſtance from their Main Army without danger of Surpriſe, and we ſhall be able to harraſs them conſtantly, and perhaps compel them to retire ſtill further.

I cannot but lament our Inability to Attack their Army and diſpoſſeſs them of New York; it appears to me of great Importance to be effeted this Campaign; at the Cloſe of it a great Proportion of our Army will be diſbanded, and the preſent State of the Country affords little Proſpeћs of Recruiting.

Z

INDEX.

LIST OF SUBSCRIBERS.

John Carter Brown, Efq., Providence, *large paper*,		1
James Lenox, Efq., New York,	do	1
William Menzies, Efq., do	do	1
Charles B. Noron, Efq., do	do	2
S. Alofsen, Efq., Jerfey City, *fmall paper*,		1
George Bancroft, Efq., New York,	do	1
Samuel L. M. Barlow, Efq., do	do	1
J. W. Bouton & Co., do	do	2
J. Carson Brevoort, Efq., Brooklyn,	do	1
Charles I. Bushnell, Efq., New York,	do	1
Enoch Carter, Efq., Newburgh,	do	1
Wm. J. Davis, Efq., New York,	do	1
H. B. Dawson, Efq., do	do	1
John Fowler, Jr., do	do	1
William H. Girard, Efq., Newburgh,	do	1
B. H. Hall, Efq., Troy,	do	1
Chas. E. Hammett, Jr., Efq., Newport,	do	1
Wm. Howard Hart, Efq., Troy,	do	1
F. B. Hough, Efq., Albany,	do	1
James B. Kirker, Efq., New York,	do	1
H. S. McCall, Efq., Albany,	do	1
John B. Moreau, Efq., New York,	do	1
T. Bailey Myers, Efq., do	do	2
Henry Nicoll, Efq., do	do	1
Charles B. Norton, Efq., do	do	5

Dr. E. B. O'CALLAGHAN, Albany, *fmall paper,*		1
SAMUEL H. PARSONS, Efq., Middletown,	do	25
Hon. G. W. PRATT, New York,	do	1
Hon. J. V. L. PRUYN, Albany,	do	1
JOEL RATHBONE, Efq., do	do	1
C. B. RICHARDSON, Efq., New York,	do	5
GEO. W. RIGGS, Jr., Efq., Wafhington,	do	1
J. RIKER, Efq., Harlem,	do	1
J. G. SHEA, Efq., New York,	do	1
J. AUSTIN STEVENS, Jr., Efq., New York,	do	1
ROBERT TOWNSEND, Efq., Albany,	do	4
FRANKLIN TOWNSEND, Efq., do	do	1
Dr. HOWARD TOWNSEND, do	do	1
Gen. FREDERICK TOWNSEND, do	do	1
W. B. TRASK, Efq., Bofton,	do	2
Hon. WM. H. TUTHILL, Tipton, Iowa,	do	1
JONATHAN N. WEED, Efq., Newburgh,	do	1
W. H. WHITMORE, Efq., Bofton,	do	1
H. AUSTIN WHITNEY, Efq., do	do	1
JOSEPH WILLARD, Efq., do	do	1
Hon. W. A. YOUNG, Albany,	do	1
Am. Antiquarian Soc., Worcefter, Mafs.,	do	1
Aftor Library, New York,	do	1
Maine Hiftorical Society,	do	1
Mercantile Lib. Affociation, Baltimore,	do	1
Military Academy at Weft Point,	do	1
New York State Library, Albany,	do	1
Wifconfin Hiftorical Society, Madifon,	do	1